Creative Display

Lynne Burgess

Bright Ideas
FOR Early Years

Published by Scholastic Ltd,
Villiers House, Clarendon Avenue,
Leamington Spa, Warwickshire,
CV32 5PR

© 1991 Scholastic Ltd
8 9 10 11 12   7 8 9

Written by Lynne Burgess
Edited by Christine Lee
Designed by Sue Limb
Illustrations by Lesley Smith
Photographs by Martyn Chillmaid

Cover photograph by Martyn Chillmaid
Printed in Great Britain by Hartnolls Ltd

British Library Cataloguing in Publication Data
A catalogue record for this book is available from the
British Library

ISBN 0-590-76506-X

Contents

Introduction

Creating a display can be extremely time-consuming and it is inevitable that many teachers, however reluctantly, will feel pressurised into giving them a low priority. The problems of fitting the National Curriculum into the limited contact time with pupils can seem daunting enough, but the thought of providing constantly changing, exciting displays can seem totally overwhelming.

This book aims to provide busy teachers with inspiration and to show how displays can be a positive aid to fulfilling many of the attainment targets in the National Curriculum. None of the ideas are meant to be slavishly copied but rather to be extended and adapted by teachers to suit their particular circumstances and, above all, to meet the needs of their pupils. It is hoped the suggestions will be used as a starting point and a means of stimulating the teacher's own ideas.

All too often display is regarded as the province of the 'artistic' teacher, whilst others feel a total lack of confidence. A good display should not rely solely on an individual teacher's ability to draw and so none of the suggestions contained in this book depend heavily upon this skill. With knowledge of a few basic techniques and a little imagination, all teachers can learn how to create successful displays. This book outlines the necessary techniques and attempts to fire your imagination!

Display in the early years classroom

Chapter one

Why display?

Obviously, there will be occasions when very young children are desperate to take home the work they have produced at school. It is very important that children can share their work with the adults in their lives. Similarly, adults should be encouraged to value their child's 'art', however primitive it may seem to them. Consequently, a display does not always have to be the ultimate goal for every art activity.

However, well-organised displays can be extremely valuable to pupils, teachers, parents and visitors for the following reasons.

• They provide a visually stimulating environment which encourages a child's natural curiosity. Not only can they inform and excite, they can also provoke questions and further exploration. It is widely acknowledged that our surroundings influence both our learning and our social behaviour.

• They can encourage in the child a positive attitude towards his surroundings. If a child can see that his work is valued by being part of a display, then he is more likely to care for that display. Hopefully, this concern will develop into a respect for the work of others and for the environment in a wider sense.

• They can develop an aesthetic awareness in pupils. Many children need to be taught to use their eyes and to appreciate the beauty in the world around them. Displays are an ideal way to increase their sensitivity and awareness, for example, of the subtle colours in a painting, the fascinating shapes in a fir cone, the dazzling reflections in a shiny kettle or the intricate patterns decorating the surface of an African clay pot.

• They can reward the child's efforts and acknowledge her achievements. Displays can be used as a means of encouraging pupils to produce their 'best' work which can then be offered as an example to others.

• They can introduce or reinforce one or more areas of the curriculum. If based on a 'theme', a display can promote further development in learning and thus be a most valuable tool to a teacher.

In the majority of schools there are two distinctive types of display, stimulus displays and pupils' displays. Both types of display can be a tremendous educational aid, supporting work in all areas of the curriculum.

Stimulus displays

The prime purpose of stimulus displays is to arouse interest and discussion, and to provoke a response. On the whole, these tend to be organised by the teacher, using objects, posters, photographs, etc.

Pupils' displays

The prime purpose of pupils' displays is to present children's work in an aesthetically pleasing manner. These displays are often organised by the teacher, using two- and three-dimensional work produced by the children. When it is appropriate, the pupils should also be involved in the decisions made during the process of setting up a display, eg arranging objects, choosing backing paper, etc.

Where to display

The positioning of displays will vary tremendously from school to school and much will depend upon the individual building. Teachers in modern purpose-built schools may well find the siting of displays much easier than those coping with Victorian buildings which were designed for a vastly different method of teaching.

The most obvious areas in which to arrange a display are in the classroom, entrance hall, corridors, assembly hall and library. Occasionally, however, it can be a useful exercise to ignore the customary sites for display and to try to view the buildings completely afresh. Is there a different area in the library which would lend itself to a display? Or another corner of the assembly hall which would be equally suitable? Often a change of situation will be enough to recapture the interest of children who, through familiarity, have become oblivious to their surroundings.

Whether the display is to be in the classroom or around the school, there are some important points to consider.

Space available

It is often difficult to find display space, especially in a small classroom which, in addition, has to provide sufficient space for a play house, sand area, quiet corner, etc. Find time to re-examine the classroom layout and see if even a small area can be made available by a more efficient use of space.

Avoid any areas where large numbers of people are constantly passing by. It is disappointing to devote a great deal of time to a display only to find it quickly becomes tatty and torn because people have rubbed against it or knocked into it.

Also bear in mind the wind tunnel effect, especially in corridors where outside doors at both ends often result in any display being damaged by draughts.

Try to retain some large empty spaces to give maximum impact to individual displays. Lots of fussy, overcrowded walls are distracting to the eye. One large focal point in an uncluttered situation can be far more effective than several small exhibitions.

Height

Always bear in mind the height of the majority of the children viewing the display and make sure that as much as possible is placed at their eye level. It is easy to forget and put labels at adult height and so make it uncomfortable for small children to read. This is particularly important to remember in narrow corridors where it is impossible for pupils to stand back far enough to see the writing on a label at the top of a display board.

Light

Good natural lighting is important to maximise the effect of any display. It is difficult to create a stimulating, attractive display in a gloomy corner with poor lighting. Sometimes artificial lighting may be necessary, but bear in mind that the wrong lights poorly positioned can cause problems with shadows and drastically alter the colours in a display. Spotlights can be used for emphasis but care must be taken to position them so as not to dazzle. If the display area is unavoidably dark and the addition of extra lights is not possible, choose light-coloured backing papers.

Safety

Obviously, you should never set up a display in front of a fire exit. Avoid blocking or narrowing a thoroughfare which may have to be used to evacuate children in an emergency. Likewise, be aware of any potential fire hazard. For example, keep any displays a safe distance from heaters, etc.

Take care to ensure that none of the objects included in a display are dangerous, eg sharp knives, toxic substances, poisonous berries or plants.

What to display

Stimulus displays

Objects

Many teachers automatically include natural objects (stones, feathers, berries, etc) in their displays, but it is also important to include man-made objects. These will be more effective if they are related to a theme. For example, a display on 'Bicycles' might include a child's bike, accessories (bell, saddle bags, stabilisers), special clothing (helmet, fluorescent safety bands, shoes), parts of a broken bike (to explore how various parts work), etc.

If possible, build up a collection of objects which can be kept centrally as a school resource bank to be used again in the future. Alternatively, borrow objects from museums, local artists and craftspeople and, above all, parents and children.

Posters

Gather together a collection of posters and, for ease of reference, organise them into themes so that any teacher wishing to find resource material on 'minibeasts' or 'metals' will be able to do so easily. *Child Education* magazine is a well-known source of suitable posters but don't forget to look out for posters in shops, building societies, etc, where they will sometimes be given away when they are no longer needed. Galleries, museums and theatres may also be willing to supply advertising posters.

Photographs

Photographs are more difficult to acquire because of the expense and the fact that they need to be fairly large. However, some teachers may feel it is worth investing in a small range of photographs whch relate specifically to their school

and local environment. For example, popular projects which appear in the curriculum on a regular basis may well be 'Our school', 'Buildings in the neighbourhood' or 'Local shops'. In these cases, large photographs of the buildings involved could be an invaluable resource.

Maps

Now that geography features as a separate subject in the National Curriculum, maps are an important resource. Large, simple, clear maps of the school buildings, the immediate neighbourhood surrounding the school or the nearest large village or town will be the most appropriate.

Works of art

Reproductions of paintings by famous artists, both past and present, are another invaluable resource. These can sometimes be bought from galleries and specialist art shops. Once again, some galleries advertise exhibitions with posters which often contain a reproduction of a famous painting and these are nearly always free upon request.

Obviously, nothing is better than displaying original works of art but these may be more difficult to obtain. They can sometimes be borrowed through Art Gallery Loan Schemes or a Schools Museum Service. It is also worth approaching local artists, and even colleges of art or secondary schools may be willing to set up a small exhibition of students' work.

Bear in mind that with some displays (seed heads, fabrics, small mechanical devices etc), it may be helpful to provide the children with devices to assist their observation, such as magnifying glasses, microscopes, mirrors etc.

In all the above, whenever possible, remember to include examples which illustrate the multicultural nature of our society. A display which includes objects derived from another culture will hopefully prompt children to be curious about a wider range of people outside their immediate family or school.

Similarly, when choosing any material for a display, avoid unintentionally reinforcing gender stereotyping. Until recently it was very difficult to find pictures and posters showing male nurses or female bus drivers but these are becoming increasingly easier to acquire.

Pupils' displays

Two-dimensional art and design can include children's paintings, drawings, prints, collage, etc. Three-dimensional art and design can include children's junk models, masks and puppets, any work in clay, Plasticine or Play-doh, any models built with construction toys (Duplo, Mobilo), etc.

Work from other areas of the curriculum can add variety and interest to a display. For example, a valuable contribution can be made by mathematics (both practical and recorded work), language (stories, poems, letters), science (both practical and written work), technology (designs and final products), geography (maps and diagrams), etc.

Effective display

Simplicity

The key to arranging a successful display is simplicity. Elaborate and overcrowded arrangements containing too many different objects, colours or textures may very well confuse rather than enhance.

Having decided which items to display, consider how best to highlight them. Try not to diminish their impact by being too fussy. The viewer's eyes should immediately be drawn to the objects or pictures central to the display and not distracted by a garish backing paper or brightly patterned drape. Always decide beforehand what is the main purpose of the display. For example, if you intend to focus the children's attention on the foliage of a selection of plants, place them against a neutral background which will not intrude on the viewer.

Obviously, all teachers need to be aware of a few basic display techniques.

Techniques associated with two-dimensional work

Trimming

Before displaying any two-dimensional work, it is essential to trim off any rough edges and any irrelevant empty spaces. Young children need to be taught to choose the appropriate size of paper for their work and then to use all of the

space available. A common feature of this age is a tiny drawing in the middle of a vast expanse of empty paper. Most pieces of work are improved by a small border of empty space around the extremities of the drawing, but if there is an imbalance in the placing of the drawing on the paper, it is acceptable to trim this excess paper off. However, before doing this, ask yourself whether the empty space adds an extra dimension to the image rather than detracting from it. For example, the empty space surrounding a small drawing could add a sense of distance or isolation which may well be appropriate for some subject matters, such as loneliness or sadness.

Types of mounting

Once the work has been trimmed, it can be stapled directly on to a display board. If a suitable backing paper has been chosen, it is not essential to mount the work again. In the interests of conservation and economy, it is increasingly important to think carefully before using vast quantities of paper. Try placing some samples of the work against a variety of coloured backing papers to discover which will be the most effective.

In some circumstances, work might benefit from single mounting. In this case, it should be stuck on to a suitable background so that a thin margin surrounds the picture. The lower margin should be slightly larger than the top one. You may prefer to 'double mount' which involves sticking the single-mounted work on to a second backing paper. However, before single or double mounting, always ask yourself whether these techniques are going to add to the work. If the framing of the work is too elaborate, the viewer will spend more time looking at the frame than the work. A delicate pencil drawing can be overwhelmed by bright or heavy double mounting.

Figure 1

Positioning

To ensure equal spacing between the pictures, work inwards from both sides of the display board. Pin the work up temporarily with the minimum number of drawing pins until you are happy with the spacing of the arrangement. Group the pictures according to subject matter or media and allow ample space between each picture. Remember that the spacing between the pictures is extremely important because it helps direct the viewer's eyes to the work.

A more interesting arrangement can be achieved if the pictures are of different sizes. This can be accomplished by offering the children a choice of size of paper before they start work and by trimming the work when appropriate.

Ensure that there is some kind of order to the display and avoid placing the pictures haphazardly on the board. Create an imaginary margin around the outside of the pictures. When placing pictures within the frame, line the edges up with the imaginary margin. Arrange smaller pictures in line with one of the edges of a larger one (Figure 1). In this way, the overall effect is deliberate and organised rather than random and so viewing the work is much easier.

There are two common errors in displaying two-dimensional work.

• Think carefully before displaying work at an angle. Even though there may be a few occasions when this is suitable, in most circumstances it distracts the eye. Most of the work being displayed has been drawn, painted or written horizontally or vertically, and to place it on a slant makes it more difficult to 'read'.

• Avoid overlapping work. It is much clearer and less confusing to be able to see the whole of each painting. Just as we would not overlap one child's poem with another's, we must also allow all of a child's composition to be viewed. There are only a few special cases (in a frieze or perhaps in a display about tessellation) where overlapping would be an advantage.

Fixing

Staples are frequently the most suitable method of fixing two-dimensional work to a display board. They are neat, unobtrusive and quick to use. The only disadvantage is that they can be difficult to extract, but this can be solved by buying a special staple remover (available from most educational suppliers).

Alternatively, double-sided tape or a loop made from adhesive tape can prove more suitable if staples are undesirable.

Adhesive spray makes single or double mounting quick and easy, but care should be taken to read the instructions regarding adequate ventilation of the room.

Whenever possible, avoid using drawing pins since their large shiny heads detract from the work being displayed. Similarly, adhesive tape used around the edges of a picture can spoil the overall effect.

Cutting out

Some purists would suggest that cutting around children's work is best avoided. In doing so, an adult often finds it difficult to resist the temptation to 'improve' the image produced by the child, sometimes altering the picture beyond all recognition. It can also ruin all the energy and spontaneity which is a vital ingredient of work by this age range.

Whether we agree with this view or not, it is worth pausing to consider why and when we do it. If the children know that their drawing is to be cut out and mounted as part of a frieze and that they don't need to include a background, then it is a more acceptable practice, provided the adult doing the cutting remains faithful to the child's work. However, there are some occasions when it may be less appropriate, such as when a child has included a background or when a child is still at the random scribble stage and incapable of producing a clearly defined image. Teachers need to be sensitive and perhaps think more carefully about the occasions when they cut around children's work.

Friezes

One of the most popular methods of displaying children's art and design work is by means of a frieze. This usually consists of a large picture which is constructed in stages, working from the background to the foreground. In this case, overlapping can be an effective way of creating depth and improving the composition.

However, with this method of display, it is easy to feel pressurised into being far too directive. If an adult has drawn the background (or sometimes the whole frieze!) and the children have merely filled this in and/or drawn round templates, what educational value has this activity had for the child? Obviously, the younger the children, the more input there has to be from the teacher, but it should be discreet and sensitive. Consider the following points when organising a frieze.

● Choose the subject matter carefully and ensure that it allows the children to work as often as possible from direct observation. Their own individual drawings of snails which they are keeping in the classroom will have far more impact than identical elephants drawn and cut out by the teacher.

● Keep the background simple and within the children's capabilities. Complicated backgrounds inevitably lead to a teacher needing to be very

prescriptive. Plain paper to which the children have added a texture, such as sponge printing or wax rubbings, will be more effective than an elaborate background drawn by the teacher. Use the backgrounds for introducing a new technique (wax resist, straw blowing) which the children can then go on to use in a more purposeful way in a future assignment. Alternatively, can the background be used to increase the children's understanding of one of the art elements (colour, shape, texture, line, pattern)? For example, how many different greens can they mix and sponge print for a grassy background?

• Gradually involve the children in more of the decisions which need to be taken when organising a frieze. Initially (and especially with very young children) you will probably need to decide the subject matter, the content, the techniques and how to mount the component parts. Discuss these aspects with the children, pointing out the reasons underlying your decisions. Once they have experienced two or three friezes, allow them to take part in more of the decision-making. Can they suggest what creatures should be included in a frieze based on the hedgerow? What technique would be most appropriate for the hedge itself? How will the hedge be fixed to the display board?

• Due to pressure of time, it is often more convenient for the teacher to mount a frieze outside the contact time with the pupils. However, whenever possible, try to involve the children in this process because it can be a useful way of learning about composition. Where should the creatures be placed on the hedgerow — in groups or singly, high up or low down? How could a large empty space be made more interesting? Will the composition be improved if some parts overlap, for example if a bee overlaps with a flower?

• Initially, it is best not to worry about scale or perspective. For example, the children will not be bothered if the snail in the hedgerow is larger than the badger. However, after a reasonable amount of experience, ask them to look for any inconsistencies in scale or perspective and once they can pick these out easily, then ask them how these could be avoided, for example by agreeing on a rough size for each item at the planning stage of the frieze, by placing larger items at the front of the picture and smaller ones at the back, etc.

Three-dimensional effects

There are occasions when even two-dimensional work can be displayed in a more interesting way by creating a three-dimensional effect. For example, in a frieze of a crowd scene, individual paintings of people could be made to look more three-dimensional by:

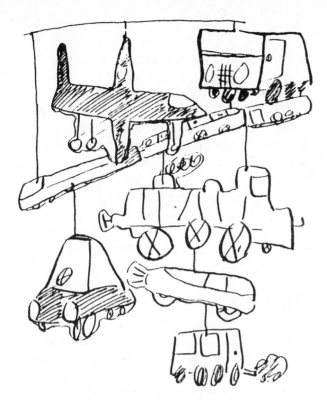

- Bending or folding the painting before stapling on to a display board;
- Using a bracket made from the piece of folded card to project the whole painting forward;
- Padding out the painted person with screwed up newspaper.

Techniques associated with three-dimensional work

Height
Display any three-dimensional work at a suitable height bearing in mind the average eye level of the children involved. Even mobiles need to be hung fairly low so that the children can easily see them.

Types of base
All three-dimensional work, whether children's art or stimulus material, is best displayed at different levels. This not only adds interest but also allows the maximum number of objects to be seen clearly.

The simplest way to achieve this without an expensive purpose-built system, is to acquire four or five strong cardboard boxes of differing sizes. These can be covered with hessian (or some other suitable fabric), corrugated card or strong sugar paper. The boxes can then be placed in an endless variety of arrangements.

If a table or cupboard top is being used as a base, conceal the top or edges with fabric, sugar paper or crêpe paper. It is also possible to create a variety of levels by using plinths. Once again, a selection of different sized boxes (or tins) can be covered with hessian, corrugated card or paper. These can then be placed on top of the table or cupboard to add height to an arrangement.

Alternatively, boxes or tins of various sizes could be placed underneath a large piece of fabric, thus creating a variety of levels as well as concealing the boxes.

Focusing
Occasionally, it might help to emphasise one item or a group of objects by placing them on:
- A circle of paper or card;
- A cork mat or tile;
- A carpet tile.

This also makes it easier for the children to return the objects to the correct position in a display where they have been encouraged to handle them.

Mobiles
Mobiles can be a very effective technique for display, especially if space is limited. They can be used for a wide range of children's work as well as information, such as vocabulary, posters and labels. Always bear in mind the height of the children. If mobiles are suspended too high, it will be

uncomfortable for pupils to look at them.

The easiest way to suspend mobiles (especially in a room with a high ceiling) is by tying black cotton to each mobile and then attaching them all to a string stretched across part of the room. However, as the mobiles are in a line, they can lose their impact.

Grouping them in small clusters can be far more effective. If the ceiling is low enough and made of a suitable material, each mobile can be pinned directly into it. Alternatively, small groups of mobiles can be tied to a hoop which is then suspended from the ceiling.

Whatever method is used to suspend the mobiles, achieving a pleasing effect often depends upon grouping them in clusters at a variety of levels.

Techniques common to both two- and three-dimensional work

Colours

As a general rule, it is wiser to avoid garish background colours and use neutral colours such as brown, grey, black, cream, pale green and pale blue. It is also more effective to put light on dark or vice versa. For example, paintings with predominantly dark colours would be better mounted on a light background whilst light-coloured shells would have more impact displayed on a dark-coloured hessian.

The background colour could echo one of the main colours in a collection of paintings or objects. It is also important to consider the overall effect of the display when choosing backing paper. For example, paintings of snow scenes are best mounted on cold colours, such as blue or grey, which reinforce the theme, whilst collages of autumn trees would be more effective mounted on a warm

autumn colour such as rust or amber. If in doubt, place the pictures against a range of colours before mounting to help you decide which will be most effective.

When choosing a colour, it is worth bearing in mind that most backing papers will fade very quickly, especially if placed near a large window. Experience of each particular display board will help you decide whether you need to compensate for this effect.

Whenever possible, recycle used backing paper.
- Turn it over!
- Use it as paper to draw on during wet play times.
- Put it in the collage box.
- Use it to practise new techniques or media, such as printing with junk items, testing out new pastels, etc.

Labelling

Labelling is important because it can be a very useful teaching aid, especially for young children. Labels can be used to increase children's awareness of print and its various functions. By drawing children's attention to the labels on a display, you can show them how print can convey a whole range of meanings from information to warnings, from instructions to amusing messages.

Labels can also be used as a vehicle to reinforce the early vocabulary contained in a reading scheme, as well as introducing new vocabulary associated with a particular topic. Encourage the children to regard the display labels as a dictionary to which they can refer when writing independently. When displaying individual drawings and paintings, write each child's name clearly at the bottom (or on a separate label) so that children can be encouraged to identify both their own names and those of their friends.

My house by Michael

The style of lettering is most likely to be that adopted by the school as a whole and contained in the reading scheme. Occasionally, the style could be altered to suit the message conveyed. For example, winter words could be written in a jagged icicle style. However, if the style is so elaborate that it interferes with clarity, then it is best avoided.

Although there may be occasions when older children are asked to help write labels, these will more frequently be done by the teacher. Black felt-tipped pen is usually the most effective because it is clear, easy to read and less likely to fade. Stencils can also be used but are slightly more time-consuming. Smaller labels could be typed by the teacher or a child using the largest print available on a word-processing program.

When writing freehand, light pencil guidelines are a very useful aid to ensure the writing is straight and that all the lower case letters are a similar size. Write the whole of the label lightly in pencil initially to make sure the spacing of the letters and words is even.

The teacher's role

The teacher plays a vital part in the effectiveness of displays throughout the school.

You are responsible for deciding how frequently the displays are changed. If a display is allowed to become tatty and dusty, then its impact on the pupils will be minimal. A stimulating and attractive environment will only be achieved if the displays are regularly changed.

You also decide the content of the display. The temptation to please parents and other adults needs to be resisted if it leads to over-prescribed friezes with minimal imput from the children. A simple display of children's drawings from observation (together with the source material which inspired them) will be far more educational, no matter how primitive their efforts may seem to adults. Use the displays to educate adults about the value of children's art.

You have to select the work which will be displayed, so ask yourself how you reach this decision. Do you always only display the 'best'? Do you display all the work to be 'fair'? Do you need to reward effort rather than attainment? Hopefully, we base our choice on each of these reasons on different occasions, but it is sometimes useful to stop and reflect upon how we have made our most recent selections. Have we got into the habit of constantly displaying the work of just a few children?

Once the display has been organised, encourage the children to interact with it. Young children are not automatically conscious of the displays around them and often pass by with nothing but a cursory glance. In order to maximise the educational potential of any display, encourage the children to spend time looking and discussing. Whenever possible, allow them to touch any three-dimensional items. Tactile experiences are vital to learning for this age group. Train the children to handle objects carefully and always to return them to the same place. Obviously, there will be occasions when the items on display will be too delicate or precious to handle, in which case devise a sign to convey this message to the children. They will quickly learn to look for this sign to know whether or not they can handle the items on display.

The display should not always be regarded as an 'end product' but sometimes as a starting point or means of developing a project further. Although very young children's responses will be mainly oral, older children could be

prompted to do follow-up work. They could draw a picture of the flowers on display, write a story inspired by a large pair of wellington boots, estimate the number of worms in a wormery, etc. Thus, the follow-up work in itself can also become part of the display.

Displays can also be used to develop the children's critical skills. Even very young children can be helped to evaluate what they see. Discuss how effective they feel the display is. Are all the objects interestingly arranged? Are the labels easily visible? What else could have been included in the display? Is the backing paper colour appropriate? Which picture (or model) do they like best and why? How could the work or the display have been improved? Obviously, the children need to be taught to be sensitive in their criticisms and to be constructive rather than destructive in their suggestions. Likewise, they will discover that agreement is not always possible, that opinions may be different without necessarily being wrong and that everyone's views should be respected.

Cross-curricular displays

With any display of pupils' work, care must be taken not to focus purely on the 'end product'. Whilst one of the aims of the art activity may well be to produce work to display in the classroom (or school), the teacher also needs to feel confident that the 'process' involves some specific art objectives. Have the children increased their skill in a particular technique or medium? Was there an opportunity to explore one of the art elements (shape, line, colour, texture, tone, pattern, etc)? Did the activity develop critical skills? It is important to remember that art has an intrinsic value and that it should not always be given a peripheral role, namely merely decorating the walls.

Apart from meeting specific art objectives, displays (both pupils' and stimulus) can reinforce other areas of the curriculum. With a little thought, displays can help even the youngest children work towards attainment targets in the National Curriculum. Far from being a superfluous luxury, displays can be a positive aid to fulfilling attainment targets across the curriculum.

The following suggestions for display include ideas for all of the core and foundation subjects in the National Curriculum, together with Religious Education. For each subject, several popular themes have been isolated and each theme contains suggestions for two displays — a stimulus display, mainly organised by the teacher, and a pupils' display, containing art and design work produced by the children.

Mathematics

Chapter two

For early years children, mathematics is a natural part of their everyday experiences and often arises spontaneously in play activities such as comparing tall LEGO structures or counting pigs in the toy farm. Displays can extend this interest and help focus attention on a particular area of mathematics such as shape, size or counting. Stimulus displays which make use of play materials help place mathematics in familiar contexts. Similarly, many art activities which contribute towards pupils' displays offer direct experiences of shapes, sizes, etc, in a meaningful and concrete way.

Large and small

Stimulus display

Age range
Any age.

What you need
Thin pink card, felt-tipped pen, strong black cotton, drawing pins, green paper, green sugar paper, adhesive tape, scissors, Playmobil playground scene, white paper, table.

What to do
Draw a large hand on a piece of thin pink card. Cut it out and use strong black cotton to suspend the hand from the ceiling.

Cover a table top with green paper (eg sugar, frieze, tissue, crêpe, etc) to represent grass. Conceal the edge of the table by cutting out a thin strip of sugar paper in the shape of a hedge, trees and a gate. Use a loop of adhesive tape to stick the hedge on to the edge of the table so that two-thirds of it protrudes above the table top.

Arrange the Playmobil playground scene (ie climbing frame, swings, bench and people) on the green paper. (Obviously, a playground scene could be made using other imaginative toys, such as LEGO, Fischer Price, etc. Similarly, the subject for the scene does not have to be a playground, but could easily be a street, a shop or a garage, depending upon the resources available.) On the wall, add a speech bubble label with a suitable caption, such as 'Help! Here comes a giant!' Position it to give the

impression that someone in the playground is shouting a warning.

Discussion

Who does the hand belong to? Is it larger than the children's hands? Is it larger than the teacher's hand? Can the children think of anything that is 'larger than' or 'as large as' the giant's hand?

Is it a male or female giant? Are there any clues?

What are the people doing in the playground? Who shouts the warning? What does the label say? Do the pupils understand the significance of speech bubbles?

How would the people in the playground feel when they looked up and saw the hand? What would they do? What would they say?

What does the giant hand do? Is the giant kind or cruel?

Use the display and the discussion points to encourage the pupils to draw sets of objects 'smaller/larger/as large as' the giant's hand. Let them make up stories based on the display. Both the 'sets' and the stories could be added to the original display at a later date.

Pupils' display

Age range
Five upwards.

What you need
Cardboard boxes of various sizes, paint, large brushes, scissors, sugar paper, stapler, PVA adhesive, collage materials (paper, tissue paper, fabric, string, etc), adhesive, corrugated card, pencils, wax crayons, white paper.

What to do
Ask the children to pile the cardboard boxes on top of one another to represent

a giant. Encourage them to experiment with different arrangements of the boxes until they find one which satisfies the majority of them. Let them paint the cardboard boxes in appropriate colours, encouraging them to consider the type and pattern of clothing.

Ask the children to suggest ways of making arms (for example, sugar paper stapled into a cylinder). Staple these in the appropriate place and stick sugar paper hands on to the end of each arm.

Encourage the children to add features to make the giant more lifelike (for example, torn paper strips for hair, paper eyes, nose, mouth, buttons, fabric scarf and belt, string for shoe laces, etc).

Cut one edge of a long piece of corrugated card to represent hill shapes. If the children want the corrugated card to be green, encourage them to use a collage technique, such as sticking on torn green tissue paper.

Grill the giant
is larger than . .
. . . . ?

Ask the children to use pencil and wax crayon to draw houses, people, vehicles, etc, then cut them out and mount them on to the corrugated card. Let them arrange the corrugated card landscape around the base of the giant.

Make a free-standing label with an appropriate caption, for example 'Gill the giant is larger than . . .'.

Discussion

Ask the children to point to the boxes which correspond to the various parts of the giant's body, such as head, shoulders, legs, feet, etc. Compare the pictures on the landscape with parts of the giant's body. Is there a child smaller than her hand? Is there a car smaller than her shoes? Is there a house as large as her head?

Use the caption to inspire a cumulative memory game. Ask one child to say 'Gill the giant is larger than' and name something appropriate from the landscape frieze. Ask a second child to repeat what the first child has said and add another example of her own. This can continue as long as desired. This game can be repeated using furniture and other objects in the room. Alternatively it can be used to reinforce the concept of 'smaller than'.

Shape

Stimulus display

Age range
Any age.

What you need
Display board covered with dark blue backing paper, different coloured sugar paper, scissors, staple gun, felt-tipped pens, rectangular tables covered with dark blue fabric, small cardboard boxes, paint, coloured card, gummed shapes, sack or postman's bag.

What to do
Cover a display board with dark blue backing paper.

Cut out a shape character (Figure 1) for each of the plane shapes being

taught. Make each shape a different colour. Staple each character to the display board and label them all with their shape name and add an overall title, such as 'The shape family'.

Place one or two rectangular tables beneath the display board and cover them with dark blue fabric. For each shape character, make a letterbox from a small cardboard box. Cut the letterbox hole into the same shape as its corresponding shape character. Paint the letterbox the same colour as the shape character.

Cut letters and postcards from different coloured card and stick on stamps made from gummed shapes, again corresponding to the shape characters illustrated on the display.

Place the appropriate letterbox on the table beneath each shape character and put the letters into a sack. Add an appropriate label, such as 'Deliver the letters to the shape family'.

Invite the pupils to post the letters and postcards into the boxes, matching the stamp shape to the correct box.

Figure 1

Discussion

Invite the pupils to look at the shape characters on the display board and guess each one's name. How many triangles can they find on the 'triangle' character? Which ones are large and which ones are small?

Explain that each member of the family has his own letterbox and ask the children to look carefully at each one. How can they tell which letterbox belongs to which character? Muddle the letterboxes up and invite individuals to put them back in the correct place.

Show the children the letters and postcards in the sack and explain that the shape of the stamp indicates which character should receive them. Allow two or three pupils at a time to deliver the letters and then let the other children check the contents of each box to make sure they have been correctly delivered. The letters can then be returned to the sack and the process repeated.

Allow the children to make their own letters and postcards with appropriately shaped stamps to add to the display.

Pupils' display

Age range
Four upwards.

What you need
Coloured card, scissors, various sized paper shapes (tissue paper, gummed paper, sugar paper, coloured foil, etc), adhesive, string or thread.

What to do
Use the above display to inspire the pupils to make their own shape character mobile. Allow them to choose which character they wish to make.

Show the children how to cut out a body shape (triangle, circle, oblong etc) from coloured card. Younger pupils may need assistance with the cutting but encourage them to decide for themselves what shape, colour and size they want. Discuss whether they are going to make a mobile using shades of one colour or several colours.

Supply paper shapes in various sizes corresponding to the body shapes. Older pupils could cut out shapes themselves, either freehand or by drawing around bricks or Logiblocs. Ask the children to stick the shapes on to their character's body to make facial features. It will probably be necessary to allow one side of the mobile to dry before sticking anything on to the other.

Challenge the children to think of a way of making arms and legs for their character. For example, strips of card can be stuck or stapled on to the body. These can be decorated with paper shapes representing feet or hands. Alternatively, show the children how to fold paper to make concertina limbs.

When the characters are dry, tie on some thin cotton and suspend them as mobiles from a line across the room or from hoops.

Discussion

What features have the children included on each character? For example, which ones have hair, eyes, nose, ears, shoes with buttons, etc? Have they remembered to add details to the back of the character? Look at several of the mobiles in detail.

Find a mobile for each shape. Can the children point out examples of large and small shapes? Can they find examples of dark and light colours?

What name would they give to their character and what sort of personality would it have? Would the shape affect the personality? For example, would a triangle character be sharp, prickly and mean?

Ordinal numbers 1 to 5

Stimulus display

Age range
Any age.

What you need
Display board covered in grey backing paper, white paper, felt-tipped pens,

tissue box, two *fromage frais* pots, two bottle tops, sugar paper, gift wrapping paper, two yoghurt pot lids, four shoe box lids, two rectangular tables covered with grey fabric, five 'set' rings, objects such as one doll, two cars, three teddies, four balls and five bricks, white card, coloured card, five paper fasteners.

What to do

Cover a display board with grey backing paper. Make a robot to staple to the display board as in Figure 1. Create a three-dimensional impression by using boxes and lids, or by bending paper, etc. Try to find materials which are attractive in themselves (for example, brightly-coloured *fromage frais* pots) so as to assemble the robot quickly. Alternatively, cover the boxes/lids with gift wrapping paper. Title the display with the robot's name, such as 'Rita Robot'. Add a speech bubble saying, 'Help me put the numbers in order'.

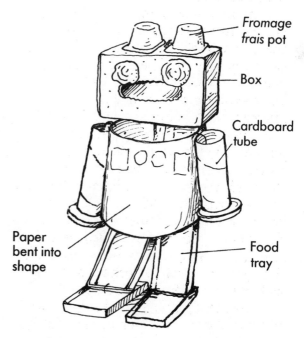

Fromage frais pot

Box

Cardboard tube

Food tray

Paper bent into shape

Figure 1

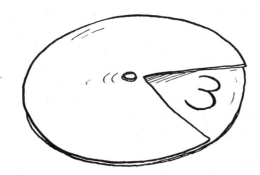

Figure 2

Place two rectangular shaped tables beneath the display board and cover them with grey fabric. Put five 'set' rings on to the tables and place objects from the classroom into them, for example one doll, two cars, three teddies, four balls, five bricks. Make a number wheel (Figure 2) for each set and place it in front of the 'set' ring.

Discussion

Introduce Rita Robot and invent some excuse for her not being able to order the numbers correctly. Look at each 'set' ring in turn, counting the number of objects and checking that the number wheel is displaying the corresponding numeral. Then change each number wheel so that an incorrect numeral is shown and invite individuals to return them to the right numeral.

Once the children are familiar with this activity, mix up the objects in the sets but leave the number wheels at their correct setting. Invite the children to return the objects to their original set.

Finally, change both the number wheels and the objects and invite children to arrange both objects and number wheels in the correct order. More able children could be asked to change the items in each set for another set of items in the room.

Pupils' display

Age range
Five upwards.

What you need
Display board covered in grey backing paper, toy robots, white paper, paint, shiny paper, scissors, adhesive, 'set' rings made from wool, string, paper, crêpe paper etc, white and coloured card, paper-clips, sharp knife, staple gun.

What to do
Encourage the children to bring toy robots from home and use them to inspire paintings of robots. Discuss their shape, colour and features such as lights, dials, buttons, etc. Invite the children to draw and paint their own robots, incorporating features from the toys.

Once the paintings are dry, offer the children shiny paper to cut and stick on for lights, buttons, etc.

Let the children cut out their robot pictures and help them to staple them on to a display board covered in grey backing paper. Group them in sets from one to five and staple a 'set' ring round them (using wool, string, paper, crêpe paper, etc).

Ask the children to suggest what each set of robots might be doing (for example, one robot buzzing, two robots flashing lights, three robots walking jerkily, etc). Write the words of each phrase on white card, but write the numeral on a separate piece of coloured card.

Staple the phrase under the appropriate set and use a sharp knife to cut a slit in the card where the numeral should go. Slip a paper-clip into the slit and slide the correct numeral card under it. The numeral cards should now be detachable.

Discussion

Count how many robots there are in each set and make sure the correct numeral is attached. Remove the cards with the numerals on, muddle them up and invite the children to return them to their correct positions. At a later stage the numeral words can be substituted (one, two, three, etc). Can the children mime the movements suggested for each set? Can they add percussion sounds for the movements?

Language

Chapter three

Promoting language development is a high priority for early years teachers and displays can be used to stimulate a variety of language experiences. Even the most reticent child can become articulate when faced with a visually exciting stimulus display or when they find their painting is part of a pupils' display. Whether concerned with geography, science or RE, all good displays offer opportunities to develop language and reading skills. A display can also highlight a particular aspect of language by developing story-telling skills, extending vocabulary or cultivating an interest in poetry.

Vocabulary

Stimulus display

Age range
Any age.

What you need
Display boxes of different sizes, display board, felt-tipped pen, white backing paper, scissors, yellow and green paper, poster(s) of leaves, brown wax crayon, staple gun, large leaves suitable for rubbings (eg sycamore or lime), a variety of foliage plants, plastic plant pot.

What to do
Arrange the display boxes to create several different levels in front of a display board covered with white backing paper.

Use the brown wax crayon to make rubbings of the sycamore leaves on pieces of green and yellow paper, leaving a space in the middle of each leaf. Cut the leaf rubbings out.

Use the felt-tipped pen to write the word 'Leaves' on to the leaf shapes, one letter in the middle of each leaf. Mount these as a title towards the top of the display board. Staple the posters of leaves underneath.

Make rubbings of the lime leaves in the same way, then write one descriptive word in the middle of each leaf rubbing (for example, spiky, variegated, pointed, hairy, curved, etc). Staple the leaves around the posters.

Arrange foliage plants on top of the boxes, choosing ones which illustrate a variety of leaves, for example:
● Large ones such as rhubarb and Swiss cheese plant;
● Small ones such as creeping fig and baby's tears;
● Plants with interesting shapes and textures, such as asparagus fern, grape ivy, holly or spider plants;
● Variegated ones such as piggy back plant, tradescantia or crotons;
● Plants with unusual colours such as coleus, pink freckle face, maranta or begonia;
● Perfumed plants such as lavender or scented geraniums.

Draw a stem on a long piece of white backing paper and pin it up as near to the display as possible. Cut out some large green leaf shapes and place them beside the empty plastic plant pot. Place a sign saying, 'Can you think of any more words to describe these plants?' near to the stem.

Discussion

Encourage the children to look carefully at a foliage plant. What shape is it? Do the leaves have unusual colours or patterns? How many variegated plants are there? Are there any prickly ones which they would prefer not to touch? Which has the largest leaves? Which has the smallest? Rub some of the leaves gently to discover whether any of them have a perfume. (Take care not to include leaves which react badly on contact with the skin.) Do any have fine hairs on the stem or leaf?

Read together the descriptive words written on the leaves mounted on the display board. Can the children think of other descriptive words? Suggest they each take a green paper leaf, write on their own descriptive word (or ask an adult to do it for them) and bring it back and put it in the empty plant pot. When there are several leaves, they can then be stuck on to the stem, starting at the bottom and working upwards. Can they think of enough words to fill the entire stem? Are there enough words to make the stem touch the ceiling?

Challenge the children to find a different leaf larger than the biggest one in the display. Similarly, can they find a plant with smaller leaves than the smallest on display? Many foliage plants also have fascinating names which reflect the character of the plant, eg spider plants or pink freckle face. Can the children invent their own names for some of the plants?

Pupils' display

Age range
Five upwards.

What you need
Low level display board at child height, posters about clothes, items of clothing, white paper, pencils, wax crayons, scissors, backing paper, staple gun, felt-tipped pen, Blu-Tack.

What to do

Using posters and real items of clothing as visual aids, discuss the fact that different clothes are suitable for different occasions. Ask some of the children to model different types of clothing – party clothes, school uniform, beach wear, ballet/gymnastic kit, etc.

Ask a group of children each to draw a large picture of one of the models from observation. Encourage them to include as much detail as possible. Suggest that they colour their drawings with wax crayons and cut them out.

Discuss which type of background would be suitable for mounting the pictures. Try holding pictures against highly decorated backgrounds and some against plain ones. Which background makes it easy to see the pictures?

Once a suitable backing paper has been decided upon, staple it to a display board and arrange the pictures on top. Add clear bold labels to each picture, naming particular garments (tie, shorts, leotard, etc). Make the labels detachable by using Blu-Tack.

Discussion

Use this display as a word bank/dictionary so that when the children are writing about clothes, they can take away any words they need to copy.

Before the children arrive at school, mix up the labels on the pictures or turn some upside down. Add a small picture of Mr. Muddle (from the *Mr. Men* books by Roger Hargreaves) somewhere on the display as a signal to the children that something is wrong. Do they notice? Can they rearrange the labels correctly?

Similarly, the labels can be used to reinforce work on phonics. Ask a child to point to all the words which begin with a particular sound. Can they name other items of clothing which begin with the same sound which are not featured in the display?

Poems

Stimulus display

Age range
Any age.

What you need
Display board covered in black backing paper, scissors, staple gun, red and pink sugar paper, felt-tipped pens, white paper for labels, food pictures from magazines, two or three display boxes (covered in black hessian, fabric or paper), food items, card for food-shaped pockets.

What to do
Cover a display board with black backing paper. Cut out a pair of giant red lips and a pale pink tongue using sugar paper. Staple the lips to the board.

Write an appropriate poem on the tongue. Eve Merriam's 'A Matter of Taste' in *There is no Rhyme for Silver* (Atheneum) is ideal. Staple the tongue to the wall, bending it to create a three-dimensional effect.

> What does your tongue like the most?
> Chewy meat or crunchy toast?
>
> A lumpy bumpy pickle or tickly pop?
> A soft marshmallow or a hard lime drop?
>
> Hot pancakes or a sherbet freeze?
> Celery noise or quiet cheese?
>
> Or do you like pizza
> More than any of these?

© Eve Merriam

Add an appropriate title to the display, such as 'What does your tongue like to taste?' Staple pictures of food from magazines around the giant mouth. Display a variety of food items on two or three display boxes in front of the board. Include tins, packets, fruit, vegetables, etc.

Invite the children to make up alliterative sentences and phrases about a favourite food. Staple some examples of your own amongst the food pictures on the display board (slippery sausages soaked in sauce, cold crunchy cucumber, etc).

Provide some paper in a food-shaped holder so that the children can write (or dictate to an adult) their own sentences about food. For example, pieces of plain paper could be provided in an apple-shaped pocket and the children could be asked to return their sentences in to a carrot shaped one. Very young children may find alliterative sentences too difficult. In this case they could dictate an interesting sentence about their favourite food, such as Ryan likes sucking wriggly spaghetti, Sarah likes crunching hard apples, etc.

Discussion

Read the poem and draw the children's attention to the words used to describe each food. Can they name other foods which are chewy, crunchy, bumpy, etc? Look at the pictures of food on the display board. Which ones do they like or dislike? Why?

Read the examples of alliterative sentences. Can they hear the dominant initial sound? Invite them to make up any sentence using words with those sounds. Look at the food displayed on the boxes and encourage them to try to make up alliterative sentences or phrases for some of the items.

Pupils' display

Age range
Five upwards.

What you need
A display board covered in dark blue backing paper, scissors, dark blue felt-tipped pens, pale blue sugar paper, white drawing paper, black or blue water-based pens or ball point pens, staple gun.

What to do
Read to the children the poem 'This is the hand' by Michael Rosen in *Mind Your Own Business!* (André Deutsch Children's Books/Armada Lions).

This is the hand
that touched the frost
that froze my tongue
and made it numb

this is the hand
that cracked the nut
that went in my mouth
and never came out

this is the hand
that slid round the bath
to find the soap
that wouldn't float

this is the hand
on the hot water bottle
meant to warm my bed
that got lost instead

this is the hand
that held the bottle
that let go of the soap
that cracked the nut
that touched the frost
this is the hand
that never gets lost.

© Michael Rosen

Discuss the poem and encourage the children to relate it to their own experiences. What have they touched today? Which things do they like or dislike touching? What else have they used their hands for today (tickling, squeezing, pointing, etc)? Invite each child to complete the phrase 'This is the hand that . . .' in a different way. This could then be written (by them or an adult) on to a hand-shaped piece of paper. Ask them to draw round their own hand on a piece of pale blue sugar paper and cut the shape out.

Ask the children to look very carefully at their own hands, focusing particularly

upon the shape and lines and creases. Suggest they draw a picture of their own hand from observation using a water-based pen or ball point pen on white paper.

Write on pale blue sugar paper a label in dark blue felt-tipped pen reading 'This is the hand that . . .'. Staple it on to a display board.

Staple the cut-out hands on to the display board. Group them together for maximum effect, for example in a fan shape, around the label in the middle of the board or from one corner.

Trim the observational drawings and staple them in the remaining space.

Discussion

Encourage the children to read the hand-shaped labels. Which one is the most interesting or amusing? Can they suggest alternatives for some of the labels? For example, instead of 'broke a new toy', what else could a hand break?

Invite the children to look carefully at the drawings of hands. Which drawings are most successful and why? Has anyone managed to draw a hand in an interesting shape, for example, with the fingers curled up or with one finger pointing? Which drawing includes the most detail? Are the lines thick/thin, straight/curved, long/short?

Songs

Stimulus display

Age range
Any age.

What you need
White paper, felt-tipped pen, dark green backing paper, paint, two display boxes covered in dark green hessian, fabric or paper, various percussion instruments (triangle, tambourine, drum, jingle bells, castanets, maracas, etc), various everyday objects which will make a variety of noises (tin, bottle, yoghurt pot, plastic lids, etc).

What to do
Choose a song which is already familiar to the children and which incorporates a variety of percussion instruments. A suitable song would be 'Oh, we can play on the big bass drum' in *This Little Puffin*, compiled by Elizabeth Matterson (Young Puffin).

On a large piece of white paper, write out the musical notation for the first phrase 'Oh, we can play on the . . .' with the words underneath. Staple this as a heading on to a display board covered with dark green backing paper.

Ask five children to paint large pictures of themselves, each playing a different percussion instrument. Cut these out and mount them on the display board under the heading. Add an appropriate label under each picture, naming the instrument being played, eg tambourine, castanets, triangle, etc.

Place two display boxes covered in dark green hessian (or fabric or paper) in front of the display board. Arrange a variety of percussion instruments on one box, such as castanets, claves, cymbal,

drum, Indian bells, jingle bells, maracas, tambourine, triangle, wood block, etc. On the other box, offer a range of everyday objects which will provide contrasting sounds, such as a tin, a bottle, plastic lids, a yoghurt pot, a plastic bag, plastic trays inside chocolate boxes, corrugated card, wooden spoons, shells, etc.

Write an appropriate label challenging the children to try making different sounds with each object. Encourage them to bang, shake, scrape, squeeze, pluck, etc.

Discussion

Draw the children's attention to the heading. Do they realise that this is how music is written? Show them a music book containing the score for familiar songs. Remind them that the heading is part of the score for a song which they know. Sing it if time allows.

Can the children recognise the instruments being played by the children in the paintings? Can they point to the corresponding percussion instrument on the display boxes? Look at each percussion instrument in turn and invite the children to play them. Group the instruments into sets, for example a set of instruments which can be shaken.

Focus the children's attention on the everyday objects. Invite them to use these to make sounds. How do they make each sound (bang, shake, tap, squeeze, etc)? Which objects can be played in more than one way? Encourage them to find other everyday objects at home which can make sounds and which can be added to the collection.

Pupils' display

Age range
Five upwards.

What you need
Display board covered in pale green backing paper, white paper, adhesive, scissors, collage materials (paper or fabric), staple gun, pale gold sugar paper, pencils, felt-tipped pens, teddy bears, table, table cloth, picnic equipment, Plasticine, picnic food, tape recorder with headphones.

What to do
Choose a familiar song which lends itself to being easily illustrated. 'The Teddy

Bears' Picnic' has been chosen for this example, but many songs are equally suitable.

Cover a display board in pale green backing paper. Discuss what kind of vegetation the children would expect to find in a wood (trees, flowers, bushes, etc). Look at real trees, bushes and flowers, if possible, and use this experience to inspire large simple drawings. Challenge the children to think of ways of using collage to decorate their drawings of trees, bushes and flowers, such as torn paper or small pieces of fabric. Cut the collage pictures out and staple them on to the backing paper to create a woodland effect.

Invite the children to make pencil drawings of teddy bears on pale gold coloured sugar paper. Encourage them to look carefully at real teddy bears whilst they are drawing so that they incorporate as much detail as possible. Cut out each bear and invite each child to decide where his bear should be stapled in the wood. Is the bear hiding behind a tree or bush? Is it climbing up a tree? Are some playing ring-a-roses? Add an appropriate label, such as 'How many teddies can you find?'

Place a table in front of the display. Cover it with a table cloth and arrange several teddy bears on it as if seated at a picnic. Put out cutlery, cups, saucers and plates, Plasticine food, etc.

Invite your class to make a tape recording of 'The Teddy Bears' Picnic' which can be placed near to the display. Add a label which encourages the audience to listen to the tape whilst viewing the picture. You may wish to provide headphones!

Discussion

Use the two-dimensional display to develop the children's understanding of positional vocabulary. Ask them to point to a bear, 'behind a tree', 'in front of a bush', 'beside a flower', 'in between a flower and a bush', etc. Reverse this activity by pointing to a particular bear and asking a child to describe its position accurately.

The three-dimensional display lends itself to a discussion about one-to-one correspondence. Has each bear got a plate, knife, fork, etc? Are there enough cakes, apples and sandwiches for all the bears?

Stories

Stimulus display

Age range
Any age.

What you need
Display board covered in pale green backing paper, scissors, staple gun, sugar paper (red, white, beige, bright green, grey, black), table, doll's house items/Playmobil accessories, felt-tipped pens.

What to do
Cover a display board with pale green backing paper. Cut from sugar paper a large toadstool with a red cap with white spots and a beige stalk large enough to draw on a door and windows. Staple this to the display board.

Cut out large grassy shapes from bright green sugar paper. Staple them around the toadstool, gathering them to create a three-dimensional effect.

Place a table covered in pale green paper immediately below the toadstool to look like a garden. Add a grey sugar paper path leading from the toadstool door.

Arrange small items in the garden outside the toadstool to look as though they had been abandoned in a hurry. Small doll's house furniture or cutlery and Playmobil accessories would all be suitable.

Cut out several giant footprints from black sugar paper and arrange them to create the impression that someone has just walked through the garden. The footprints can be stapled to the display board and stuck on to the garden.

Add a question mark shaped label with the words 'Who lives here? What has happened to them?'

Discussion
Use the display to inspire the children's imagination. Who do they think lives in the toadstool house? What size are they? What could they have been doing before the visitor arrived? How would they have felt when the visitor arrived? What was the visitor like? What do the footprints tell you? Was the visitor kind or unkind? Encourage the children to invent a sequence of events both in the past and in the future.

This activity could be a purely oral story-telling experience, with a group, class or individual story being constructed. Alternatively, after discussion, pupils could be asked to write their own story. (Younger children could dictate theirs to an adult.) All the stories could then be made into a class anthology which could become part of the display.

Pupil's display

Age range
Five upwards.

What you need
Light blue backing paper, turnip, white paper, paint, felt-tipped pens, string, yellow tissue paper, adhesive, staple gun.

What to do
Choose a story which is familiar to the children. The example used here is *The Great Big Enormous Turnip* by Leo Tolstoy (Picture Lions), but many other stories would be equally suitable. Cover a display board with light blue backing paper.

Ask a child to mime pulling up a turnip and draw the children's attention to the shape of the body and position of the limbs (especially arms). Repeat the activity with another child miming trying to push the turnip.

Divide the children into two groups and ask them to paint a picture of themselves either pushing or pulling up the turnip. Show them the display board which is to be used and discuss how they intend to paint the arms. Cut out the finished paintings.

Invite two or three children to help make the turnip. Look at a real turnip and focus the children's attention on the colour and texture. Can they suggest ways of depicting these? For example, thick string could be stuck on to the turnip shape to indicate the texture whilst various shades of yellow tissue paper could be stuck over the top. The tissue could be overlapped to create slightly different shades.

Staple the turnip and the paintings of children on to the display board. Tilt some of the paintings to make it look as if the children are all about to fall over. Add a suitable heading, such as 'Up popped the great big enormous turnip'. Speech bubbles can also be added, such as 'Push!', 'Pull!' and 'Help!' from a small

Up popped the great big enormous turnip

child at the back about to be squashed as they all fall over.

Discussion

Use the frieze to reinforce concepts of more than and less than. How many children are pushing? If one sat down for a rest, how many would be left? How many are pulling? If one more child came to help, how many children would there be altogether?

Ask the pupils to invent speech bubbles for some of the other children. What would they be thinking or saying?

Science

Chapter four

Science displays, perhaps more than any others, are most successful when they are interactive and allow the children to touch and explore the objects involved. Displays which invite the children to investigate or which involve activities which improve their observational skills can be powerful tools for learning.

Weather

Stimulus display

Age range
Any age.

What you need
Display board, grey backing paper, staple gun, scissors, coloured paper in black, orange, yellow, blue and white, two or three cardboard boxes, grey hessian or another appropriate material, items associated with various types of weather.

What to do
Cover a display board with grey backing paper. Cut out a large black cloud and add the word 'Weather', each letter cut from coloured paper, using colours ranging from hot to cold tones. For example, We – orange, at – yellow, he – blue, r – white. Staple the letters on to the cloud shape as a heading.

Write a label asking 'What do you like to do in the . . .?' and then individual labels for 'sun', 'rain', 'wind' and 'snow'.

Cut out a large simple symbol to represent each different kind of weather, for example a sun, an umbrella, a kite, a snowman. Write a related activity on each symbol, such as 'swim in the sea', 'splash in the puddles', 'chase after leaves' or 'throw snowballs'. Staple the symbols on to the display board with the appropriate label.

Place two or three cardboard boxes (covered in grey hessian, fabric, corrugated card or paper) in front of the display board. Group items associated with each kind of weather on the boxes, such as an inflatable swimming ring, a bucket, a spade, shells, sunglasses to represent the sun; an umbrella, a rain hat and boots to represent rain; a kite and a toy windmill to represent wind; a sledge, a bobble hat, a scarf and gloves to represent snow.

Discussion
Discuss the pictures on the display board. What sort of weather do the pupils think each picture symbol could denote? Read the label on each picture and encourage the children to suggest alternative activities suitable for each different weather condition. Which type of weather do they like best and which do they like least? Why?

Look at the items on the display boxes. Can they name and describe each item (colour, shape, material, purpose, etc)? Which type of weather would each object belong to? Ask the children to close their eyes whilst you remove several of the objects. Can they identify which objects have been removed? Invite a child to allocate each object to the appropriate group or set. What other objects could have been included in each set?

Pupils' display

Age range
Four upwards.

What you need
Large sheets of pale grey sugar paper, watering can, chalks, paints, white paper, pencils, wax crayons, strips of polythene, cork tile, card, children's rainwear, scissors, staple gun.

What to do
The following example is concerned with rainy weather but a similar frieze could be developed for other types of weather. After discussion with the children, decide upon a scene for the frieze, for example in the street, in the playground, at the park, etc. If a street scene has been chosen, discuss what the children might expect to see there and how rainy weather would affect the scene. If possible, go and observe a street in the rain. Alternatively, use a watering can to make artificial puddles in the playground for the pupils to observe.

Ask one group of children to make chalk drawings of rain clouds on large pieces of grey sugar paper. Encourage them to smudge the colours together.

Invite another group of children to paint puddles on wet grey sugar paper so that the colours blur.

A third group of children could paint large pictures of houses and cut them out. If possible, let them look at some real houses before painting their pictures.

Ask two or three children to dress up in their 'rainy' clothes to provide a focus for discussion. Each child could then draw a large picture of themselves in the rain, colour it with wax crayons and cut it out.

Staple the cloud and puddle pictures on to the display board. If possible,

arrange for the children to help decide where to staple the houses and the people.

Invite the children to suggest how the effect of rain coming down could be achieved. Possible techniques could be painting with a brush, printing with a thin card or piece of cork tile, stapling strips of polythene, etc.

Once the frieze has been mounted, add an appropriate label on a grey sugar paper puddle shape, for example 'We are splashing in the puddles'.

Discussion

As often as possible, use direct experiences to inspire each group's work. Look out of the window at rain clouds, take the children outside to observe puddles and study buildings and ask one or two children to wear their outdoor clothing and hold umbrellas.

Before working on the clouds and puddles, ask the children which colours they think would be most appropriate. Encourage them to blend one colour with another and watch to see what happens when two colours mix.

Discuss mounting the frieze with the children. Should the houses be placed in a row or in groups? Would it be more

effective to leave different sized gaps in between them? Does it matter if the people overlap the houses? Would they look more three-dimensional if their arms, legs and bodies were bent whilst being stapled to the board? How should the people be grouped? Where would be the best place to put the label?

Push and pull

Stimulus display

Age range
Any age.

What you need
Display board covered in green backing paper, display box covered in green hessian, scissors, fabric or paper, white paper, red paper, light green paper, paper in a variety of other colours, felt-tipped pens, small box, wrapping paper, cardboard tube, thick card in white and blue, adhesive, adhesive tape, stapler, hole punch, string, three small metal hooks, selection of toys to illustrate pushing (lorry, train, pop-up toys, pushchair, wheelbarrow, etc) and pulling (pull-along animals or vehicles, stringed puppets, etc).

What to do
Cover a display board with dark green backing paper and a display box with dark green hessian, fabric or paper. Staple a heading on to the display board, such as 'Push and Pull'.

The following instructions describe four simple push and pull activities which could be displayed to foster an understanding of this theme. They are meant to be touched and therefore need to be made from thick card and displayed at child height. These are merely examples. You may wish to develop and/or extend one idea as well as adapting the subject matter to suit your pupils' needs.

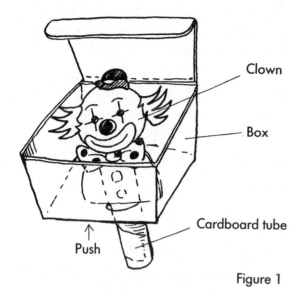

Clown

Box

Cardboard tube

↑ Push

Figure 1

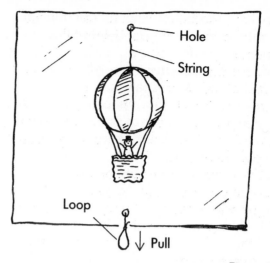

Hole

String

Loop

↓ Pull

Figure 2

• Make a pop-up clown by covering a small box with wrapping paper, allowing the lid to open freely. Insert a short cardboard tube into the base of the box so that it will slide easily up and down. Draw a simple clown's face on thick card, colour it with felt-tipped pens, cut it out and stick it on to the end of the cardboard tube. The clown should not be visible until the cardboard tube is pushed upwards (Figure 1). Staple the box firmly to the display board.

• Make a hot air balloon. Punch a hole at the bottom and top of an oblong-shaped piece of thick blue card. Draw a simple hot air balloon shape on white card, colour it with felt-tipped pens and cut it out. Stick a long piece of string on to the back of the balloon. Thread the string through the top hole, behind the card and out through the bottom hole. Staple the whole piece of card firmly to the display board. Tie a loop in the string at the bottom. As the string is pulled, the balloon should rise to the top of the card (Figure 2).

• To make a butterfly, cut an appropriate sized piece of thick blue card into an oblong. Cut another thin strip of the same card so that it is approximately 20cm longer. Cut two vertical slits in the card so that the thin strip of card will slide easily in them. Slide the card into place. Draw a butterfly on thick card, colour it with felt-tipped pens and cut it out. Staple it on to the thin strip of card. Reinforce both ends of the strip of card by sticking on extra pieces of card. These should be slightly larger than the strip to prevent the strip being pulled out. Staple or stick on several paper flowers at the bottom of the piece of blue card. Staple the whole piece of card firmly on to a display board. As the thin strip of card is pulled, the butterfly should move towards the flowers (Figure 3).

→ Pull

Strip of card

Figure 3

● To make a ladybird, cut out a large light green leaf shape. Use felt-tipped pens to add leaf veins. Staple it on to the display board. Draw a ladybird on thick card, colour it with felt-tipped pens and cut it out. Screw three small circle-shaped hooks through the leaf into the display board in a triangular pattern. Thread string through each hook and tie it to form a continuous loop. Stick the ladybird on to the string at point A (Figure 4). Add a string handle at point B to make it easier for children to operate. As the handle is pulled, the ladybird should move up the leaf.

Add red arrows to the display, labelled 'Push' or 'Pull' as appropriate.

Display toys which can be pushed and/or pulled on the display box. Add a

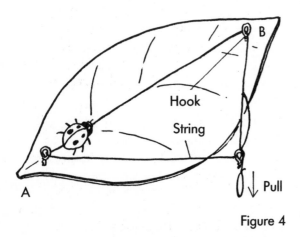

Figure 4

suitable caption, such as 'Which toys can be pushed?' or 'Are there any which can be pulled?'

Discussion

Read the heading with the children and then discuss each component of the display in turn. Point out the 'push' and 'pull' arrows and demonstrate how to operate each activity. Warn the children to do each activity gently. Can they predict what might be in the box? What do they think is going to happen when the cardboard tube is pushed? Can they guess what might happen when the strings or card are pulled? Allow them to take turns using each activity. Do they realise that, in order to return an activity to the beginning, they often have to make the opposite movement? For example, they push to make the clown pop up, but pull to make it return inside the box.

Look at the toys displayed on the box. Invite individuals to find a toy which is pushed (or pulled) and to demonstrate how it works. Can they name other similar toys? Make a collection of toys from home and sort them into 'push' and 'pull' sets.

Pupils' display

Age range
Four upwards.

What you need
Display board covered in a neutral colour, small boxes, cardboard tubes, wrapping paper, white card, thick card, string, hole punch, adhesive tape, staple gun, white paper for heading, felt-tipped pens or wax crayons.

What to do
Discuss the construction of the two simplest activities on the stimulus display board, the pop-up clown and the hot air balloon. Suggest that the children use the basic construction method to make a toy of their own. Allow them to choose which one they wish to make. Encourage them not to copy the display identically but to think of their own subject matter. What could pop up out of the box apart from a clown? They may suggest a monster, spider, mouse, teddy, etc. What else could be pulled up by a string? They

Come and try our push and pull toys

might suggest a butterfly, bee, aeroplane, bird etc.

Older or more able children may wish to alter or improve upon the basic construction method and this should be encouraged.

Cover a display board with a neutral colour and staple the children's constructions to the board. Add an appropriate label, such as 'Come and try our push and pull toys' together with 'push' and 'pull' arrows.

Discussion

Can individuals describe the construction process in sequential order to the other children? What materials and equipment did they need? Older children could make a list. Were there any difficulties in the construction and how did they overcome these? How well do their push and pull toys work? Could they be improved by using an alternative material, for example thicker card?

If the results of this activity are displayed and the children are encouraged to try out each other's toys, an ideal opportunity presents itself for discussing care and respect for other people's work. How would they feel if their work were damaged through someone else's carelessness? What 'rules' could they suggest for pupils using this particular display?

Magnets

Stimulus display

Age range
Any age.

What you need
Display board covered with black backing paper, staple gun, white paper, felt-tipped pens, pictures of things which are attracted to magnets, two display boxes covered with black hessian, fabric or paper, small cardboard box, white card, paper-clips, a variety of magnets (different shapes, sizes, strengths), a

collection of everyday objects (some of which are attracted to magnets and some not).

What to do

Cover a display board with black backing paper. Cut out a large horseshoe magnet shape in card and write the title 'Magnets' on it. Staple it to the display board.

Cut pictures from magazines illustrating a variety of things which are attracted to magnets and staple them to the ends of the giant magnet.

Place two display boxes (covered with black hessian, fabric or paper) beneath the display board.

Cut a small cardboard box as shown in Figure 1. Draw a large grandfather clock on a piece of card and stick it over the front of the box. Add the title 'Hickory Dickory Dock' to the top. Cut out several mice from thin card and fix a paper-clip to each one. Place the clock, mice and several different magnets (various shapes, sizes, strengths) on one of the display boxes. Add an appropriate label, such as 'Can you use the magnets to make the mice climb up the clock?'

On the other display box, arrange a variety of objects and challenge the

children to use the magnets to find out which are attracted to the magnets.

Discussion

Look at the cardboard horseshoe magnet on the display board. Can the children find an example of a real one in the collection of magnets? Are all magnets this shape? Discuss the significance of the pictures stapled to the ends of the magnet on the display board.

Allow the children some time to experiment, then discuss the collection of objects on the display box. Can the pupils say which objects are attracted or not attracted to the magnets? Do the objects stick to the whole of the magnets or only part of them? Can the pupils use the magnets to make the mice climb up the clock? Which part of the magnet do they use? Is it easier with some magnets than others?

Challenge them to see if they can move the mice with the magnets through other materials, such as wood, hardboard, plastic, foil, tracing paper, etc. Can they think of everyday uses for magnets? Perhaps they could make a collection of objects or pictures which illustrate the use of magnets, such as toys, games, door-catches, tin-openers, etc.

Figure 1

Pupils' display

Age range
Four upwards.

What you need
Small cardboard box, vase of flowers, pale green card, scissors, adhesive, white card, paper-clips, variety of magnets, felt-tipped pens, blue sugar paper, fishing rods with magnets, display box covered in blue hessian (fabric or paper).

What to do
Cut a small cardboard box as shown in Figure 1. Ask two or three children to draw flowers on a piece of pale green card to be stuck to the front of the cardboard box. Provide a small vase of real flowers to inspire their drawings.

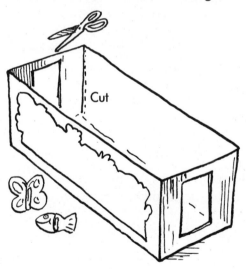

Figure 1

Ask the children each to draw, colour and cut out a butterfly. Fix a paper-clip to each one.

Place the box and the butterflies on a display box. Supply a variety of magnets and invite the pupils to make their butterflies move from flower to flower.

Place a piece of sugar paper cut into the shape of a pond in front of the flowers. Ask the children each to draw, colour and cut out a fish. Let them fix a paper-clip to each one and place them in

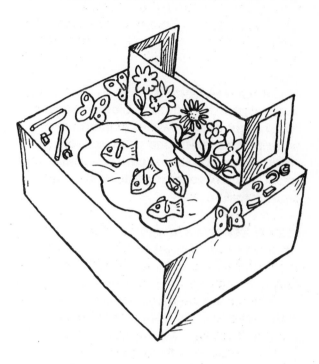

the pond. Supply fishing rods with magnets to catch the fish. Let the children stick coloured labels on the fish or write on numbers and devise an appropriate game.

Discussion
Can the children make the butterflies move? Which magnet is easiest to use? Can they catch the fish with the rods? Can they invent a game using the fish? For example, can they catch all the fish with the same coloured sticker underneath or all those with number 3 on them? Can the children suggest an alternative to paper-clips, such as paper-fasteners? Try out their suggestions to discover which work best. Older children may be able to devise their own games involving magnets.

Eyes

Stimulus display

Age range
Any age.

What you need
Display board covered in blue backing paper, light brown, white, pink and red sugar paper, felt-tipped pens, scissors, staple gun, small table covered in blue paper with crêpe paper frill, white card, toothpicks.

What to do
Cover a display board with blue backing paper and add the title 'Eyes'. Cut out two eyebrow shapes from light brown paper. Use felt-tipped pens to draw two large eyes on white paper and cut them out. Cut out a pink nose and red lips. On the lips, write the words: 'Do your eyes play tricks on you?' Staple all these features to the display board to form a face. Fold and bend the nose to give a three-dimensional effect.

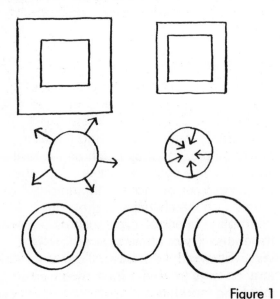

Figure 1

Draw a series of simple optical illusions on white paper and staple them at the bottom of the board. Some examples are shown in Figure 1. Although the shapes are the same size, they can appear larger/smaller according to the lines around them. Add an eye-shaped label: 'What do you see?'

Cover a small table with blue paper and add a blue crêpe paper frill. Place the table near to the display board.

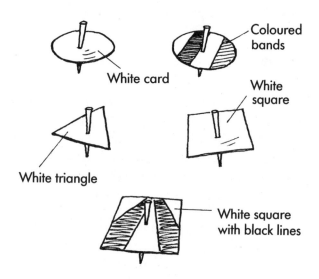

White card
Coloured bands
White square
White triangle
White square with black lines

Figure 2

Make a series of spinners with white card and toothpicks pushed through the centre. Examples are given in Figure 2. Add an eye-shaped label: 'Spin and watch what happens'.

Discussion
Before looking at the display in detail, ask the children if they think their eyes do play tricks on them. Suggest they study the optical illusions and describe what they can see. Do they realise the shapes are, in fact, the same size? Have a cardboard circle and square of the same size available so that pupils can hold

What to do

Show the pupils some examples of half masks and invite them to design one of their own. Older pupils may well be able to draw their designs before making them. Suggest the pupils try to use their designs to convey a particular emotion. For example, can the mask help to portray sadness or anger?

To decide the width of the mask, measure the face from ear to ear and cut a rectangular piece of card to that size. Ask the children to fold the card in half and draw the outline shape of the mask. These can be as complex as they wish. Cut out the mask and the eyeholes. Younger pupils will need assistance with the eyeholes.

Provide a range of collage materials with which the children can decorate their masks. When the masks are dry, show them how to fasten on some elastic ties. Again, younger pupils will need help with this. An example of a mask is given in Figure 1.

them over each illusion to compare sizes easily. Before using the spinners, encourage them to predict what they think they might see. Once they have had time to use the spinners, ask them to describe exactly what they see with each one. Did anyone predict correctly? Can anyone offer an explanation? The children might like to experiment by making their own spinners using different shapes and colours.

Pupils' display

Age range
Four upwards.

What you need
Examples of half masks, display board covered in dark green backing paper, tape measure, scissors, different coloured thick card, elastic, collage materials (tissue paper, crêpe paper, foil, string, wool, raffia, sequins, gummed paper, glitter, etc), adhesive.

Figure 1

Display the masks on a board covered with dark green backing paper. Add a mask-shaped label, such as 'Wear a mask and change your eyes'. Let the children use their masks in dance/drama activities.

On the masks: "wear a mask / change your eyes"

Discussion

How does the shape of the mask help convey an emotion? For example, does a sharp spiky shape make the children think of anger or happiness? Would the colour of the collage materials also affect the emotion being expressed, for example red for anger, blue for sadness? Suggest that some of the children try on their masks whilst the others watch. How do the masks alter their faces? Does a half mask make the eyes the focus of attention more than a whole mask? How do the pupils feel when wearing their masks? What can they see and how much does the mask alter their field of vision?

Technology

Chapter five

Technology is a subject which spans the curriculum and offers endless possibilities for display. A stimulus display can be used as a vehicle for exploring materials or identifying needs whilst many of the pupils' own designs and final products easily lend themselves to visual presentation.

Houses (materials)

Stimulus display

Age range
Any age.

What you need
Display board covered with grey backing paper, builder's wheelbarrow, sacking or polythene, large poster of a house, green sugar paper for labels, samples of house building materials (metal, glass, wood, plastic, clay, etc).

What to do
Cover a display board with grey backing paper. Add a suitable heading on green paper, such as 'Which materials are used to build a house?' Staple a large poster of a house in the centre of the board. Cut out five house-shaped labels, each with the name of a different material written on it, ie metal, glass, wood, plastic, clay. Staple these around the poster. Place the wheelbarrow beneath the display board.

Display as many examples as possible for each material, based on a 'house-building' theme. Arrange the objects in and around the wheelbarrow, draping sacking or polythene to provide a background surface for smaller items. Metal items could include nails, screws, door and window furniture; glass items could include window panes (but consider safety); wood items could include pieces of timber (various sizes), window frames, parts of floorboards or skirting boards; plastic items could include guttering, pipes, door furniture and electrical fittings, such as switches and sockets; clay items could include bricks, floor, wall and roof tiles, chimney pots, etc.

Add an appropriate label, such as 'Where would these materials be used?'

Discussion
Read the main heading and each of the 'house-shaped' labels. As each label is read, ask the children to point to examples of that material in the display. Encourage them to touch each material and describe its texture, colour, etc. Why is that particular material most appropriate for that purpose? Encourage them to think about strength, transparency, durability, flexibility, whether it is waterproof, etc. Can the children suggest an alternative, yet equally acceptable material? For example, door furniture can be metal or plastic. Invite individuals to explain whereabouts in a house each item would most likely be found. Use the poster to clarify any difficulties. For example, some children may never have noticed the guttering before.

Pupils' display

Age range
Five upwards.

What you need
White paper, pencils, paint, sponges, collage materials, adhesive, display board covered in light blue backing paper, small cardboard boxes, card, two display boxes covered in light blue hessian, fabric or paper.

What to do
Use the story of the Three Little Pigs as a basis for a frieze.

Organise a group of children to draw three pigs and decorate them with sponge prints, while another group uses collage materials to make three houses.

Mount the pigs and the houses on a display board covered with light blue backing paper. Add a speech bubble to each pig with the name of each material on it (ie straw, sticks and bricks). Add an appropriate label, such as 'Which little pig used the best material?'

Arrange for a group of children to make houses out of cardboard boxes. Direct observation of real houses will help them to add realistic details and move away from the standard box with one door and four windows.

Cover two display boxes with light blue hessian, fabric or paper and arrange the cardboard houses on them. Older children could be encouraged to list the materials they would use if they were building a real house.

Discussion
Which of the Three Little Pigs' houses was built of the most appropriate material and why? What materials and/or techniques have the children used to show a house made of bricks, straw and sticks?

Look closely at the cardboard houses. Which ones include interesting details, such as guttering, porches, windowsills, etc? Which materials have been used on the models and which would be used in real houses? What would be the disadvantages of living in a house made from cardboard?

Clay (process)

Stimulus display

Age range
Any age.

What you need
Several display boxes covered in dark green hessian, soft clay, rolling pin, cling film, a shallow biscuit tin lid, tools for creating impressions in clay, a shallow plastic tray, one unfired pot, picture of a kiln, one fired pot, collection of objects made from clay (unglazed), yellow paper, felt-tipped pens, white paper for labels.

What to do
Roll out some coils of clay to form the word 'Clay'. Impress a different texture into each letter using junk materials. If this is done inside a shallow biscuit tin lid, it will be easier to display. Position the title at one end of a series of stepped display boxes covered in dark green hessian as in the illustration.

Wrap a piece of clay in cling film (so that it will not dry out) and display it with a label saying, 'Soft clay. Where does it come from?' Add a yellow paper arrow pointing to the next item.

Roll out a piece of damp clay, place it in a shallow tray and use five or six different tools/implements to make indentations in it. Display the clay together with the tools and add a label saying 'Which tools made each mark?' Add a second yellow arrow.

Place an unfired pot, a picture of a kiln and a fired pot on the display box in that order with arrows to help pupils follow the process. Add a label: 'How has the clay changed?'

Place another yellow arrow pointing to a collection of objects made from unglazed clay, such as bricks, tiles, flower pots, chimney pots, etc.

If the children have had experience of using glazes, another section could be

added to the display comparing glazed and unglazed objects.

Discussion

Emphasise that the pupils need to follow the yellow arrows to gain an appreciation of the process of making something with clay.

Let them touch the clay wrapped in cling film. What can we do with soft clay (pinch, press, squeeze, roll it, etc)? Can they match the tools to the impressions in the clay?

If there is a kiln available in the school, show it to the pupils, explain how it works and relate it to the picture of a kiln. How does firing in a kiln change the clay? Can the children identify the objects in the collection? Perhaps they could find examples at home to add to the collection.

Pupils' display

Age range

Five upwards.

What you need

Clay (raku or any other low-firing clay), modelling tools, drying-out boards, an old metal dustbin plus lid, sharp implement for making holes, fine sawdust, firelighter, display boxes covered in dark red hessian, display board covered in dark red backing paper, white paper, pencils, wax crayons, plinths (small boxes covered in dark red hessian).

What to do

Give each child a small lump of clay (raku is best but any other low-firing clay should work). Ask the children to pat the clay into a sphere, smoothing any cracks with their fingers.

Show them how to push their thumbs gently into the centre of the sphere and pinch the walls evenly, turning the sphere as they work. Encourage them to work with the sphere in their hand and not on the table, otherwise they will squash it flat against the table.

Offer the children modelling tools to add lines or textures to their pots.

Place the finished pots on a board and dry them out slowly.

Make a sawdust kiln to fire the thumb pots. Find a sheltered site away from the school and not easily accessible to other children. Choose a day when it is not windy.

Punch holes approximately 1cm in diameter and at 15cm intervals into an old metal dustbin to allow ventilation for even burning. Place a 10cm layer of fine sawdust in the bottom of the dustbin and then stand the pots in the centre, leaving a 10cm gap at the edge.

Cover the pots well with sawdust (at least 8cm) and then repeat layers of pots and sawdust, finishing with a 15cm layer of sawdust at the top.

Light a firelighter on top of the sawdust

and allow the sawdust to smoulder gently. Use the lid to control the draught by putting it on tightly if the sawdust is burning too quickly. It will probably smoulder for two days and should then be allowed to cool naturally before removing the pots. Extreme caution must be taken as the outside of the dustbin does become quite hot. Make sure that the children do not go near the dustbin during the firing process.

Remove the pots from the dustbin and wash them. They will be various shades from grey to black, possibly with some iridescent colouring.

Display the children's thumb pots on two display boxes, covered in dark red hessian. Use plinths to create a variation in height.

Organise a group of children to work in pairs, drawing large pictures (pencil and wax crayon) to show the process of making and firing their thumb pots. Display these pictures on a board covered in dark red backing paper. Add appropriate labels to describe the process.

Discussion

Look carefully at the finished thumb pots and ask the pupils to describe them in detail, commenting on features such as colour, texture, shape, etc. Read through the descriptions of the processes for making a thumb pot and firing a sawdust kiln. Has anything important been forgotten? Are the instructions clear and easy to read? Would the pupils be able to follow these instructions if they had never done this before?

Shops (satisfying needs)

Stimulus display

Age range
Any age.

What you need
Display board covered in grey backing paper (at child height), white paper, strong white card, felt-tipped pens, small table, staple gun, scissors, old magazines.

What to do
Cover a display board with grey backing paper. Draw three or four large, simple shop fronts on white paper. Write the name of the type of shop as a sign at the top. Staple each shop on to the display board.

Cut a piece of card to form a pocket to be stapled over the front of each shop.

Draw (or cut from magazines) simple pictures of goods sold in each shop and stick them on to card. Colour the drawings with felt-tipped pens and cut them out.

Place the cards on a table near the display and invite the children to put the goods into the correct pocket for each shop.

Discussion
Have the children ever been inside these kind of shops? What does each one sell? What other kind of shops do they know and what sort of goods would they expect to be able to buy in each? Can they match the cards supplied to the correct shop? Suggest that they draw their own pictures of different goods to be added to the cards supplied by the teacher.

If the children enjoy this activity, they may wish to add other shops or replace those already on the frieze.

Pupils' display

Age range
Five upwards.

What you need
A collection of advertising posters, paper in a variety of sizes, shapes and colours, pencils, felt-tipped pens, paint, wax crayons, display board covered in grey backing paper.

What to do

Show the pupils several posters used to advertise goods in shops. Discuss their design and layout in detail. Are there any pictures? How much text is there and what information does it convey? Which parts of the text are large and which parts are small? Why? What colours have been used? Why?

Use the examples of posters and the discussion to inspire the children to design their own posters, perhaps linked to a specific shop on the stimulus display. Which particular product do they want to advertise? Is there a special reason for advertising it (such as the price of the product being reduced or a particular fruit having just become seasonally available)? The children may wish to make a rough draft before starting on a full-sized poster.

After some discussion, offer the children paper in a variety of shapes, sizes and colours. Encourage them to draw their design lightly in pencil so that alterations can easily be made.

Discuss the advantages and disadvantages of various media for their advertisements. Felt-tipped pens are probably the most appropriate media for making posters but some pupils may wish to use paint or wax crayons.

Display the posters on a board covered in grey backing paper. Group them together according to subject matter.

Discussion

Look carefully at the final posters and discuss how successful they have been. Which ones are easy to read from a distance? Which catch your eye immediately and why? Are some colours more striking than others? Does the background colour of the paper make any difference to the success of the poster? Do unusually shaped posters make more impression than ordinary rectangular shaped ones?

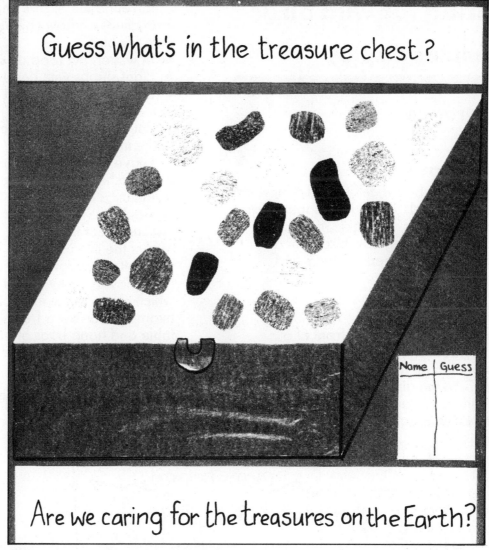

Guess what's in the treasure chest?

Name | Guess

Are we caring for the treasures on the Earth?

Geography

Chapter six

Many aspects of geography can be presented to young children through displays. Maps are an obvious subject for display but both physical and environmental geography can provide an exciting focus, for example, by examining animals, birds and plants or by highlighting an environmental issue such as litter.

Caring for wild birds

Stimulus display

Age range
Any age.

What you need
Display box, board, felt-tipped pen, white paper for labels, blue sugar paper, poster about wild birds, bird table, nuts, bird cake, food, nesting box, bird bath or dustbin lid, seed heads, flowers and berries.

What to do
Position a display box in front of a display board. Use the board to provide information on how to help care for wild birds. Title the display 'Please help me' (or something similar) and put up a poster or picture depicting wild birds.

Surround the picture with brief instructions on how children can help care for birds.
- In winter, put food on a bird table.
- Plant shrubs with berries for me to eat.
- Leave dead flowers to seed for me to eat.
- Put out water for me to drink and bathe in.
- Leave my eggs and chicks alone.
- Keep hedges for me to shelter in.
- Put up a nesting box.
- Don't kill winter moth caterpillars because I eat them.

Mount the instructions on bird-shaped silhouettes cut from blue sugar paper.

Display as many items as possible which relate to the instructions. For example, borrow a free-standing bird table and hang bags of nuts on it; show examples of suitable food (bread soaked in water, cheese, fat, fruit, a bird cake plus the recipe); put twigs from shrubs with berries (hawthorn, elder, pyracantha) and seed-bearing flowers

(sunflower, marigold, Michaelmas daisy) into a vase; show the appropriate nesting box; display a bird bath (or upturned dustbin lid supported on bricks to make it level) etc.

Discussion

Can the children identify the birds on the poster? Have they ever seen any of them? Where?

Help them to read the title and ask them why we need to help wild birds. What time of year are they particularly vulnerable?

Read each instruction and ask the children to say which items on display relate to them.

What contribution do wild birds make to our lives?

Pupils' display

Age range

Five upwards.

What you need

For the background: grey sugar paper, white paint in a tray such as an ice cream container lid, newspaper, sponges, brown paint, brushes, adhesive. For the birds: white paper, paint in individual trays, junk items such as corks, cotton reels, corrugated card, thick cardboard, off-cuts of balsa wood, scissors.

What to do

Print a snowy background by using sponges and screwed up newspaper dipped in white paint and pressed on to the grey sugar paper. Use white marks to indicate snowflakes falling and snow-covered ground.

Ask one or two children to paint a large bird table to be stuck on to the snowy background. Encourage them to

look carefully at the bird table in the display.

If possible, use the children's firsthand observations of birds feeding at a bird table to inspire individual pictures of birds. Suggest each child draws a large outline of a common wild bird, but don't insist if some feel confident to print without one.

Use the junk items to print shapes and textures on to the bird outline to indicate feathers, eyes, beak, claws, etc.

When dry, cut out the birds and mount them on and around the bird table.

Discussion

If possible, involve the children in composing the picture. Initially pin the bird table and birds on to the background so that alternatives can be considered. Is it better to have the bird table in the middle or to one side? Should all the birds be on the ground, on the bird table or in the sky? Consider the size of the birds. Should the large ones be in the foreground and the smaller ones in the background? Are there any large empty spaces? If there are, can the children suggest what to do with these?

Litter

Stimulus display

Age range
Any age.

What you need
Large strong boxes, one cuboid shape, one cube shape, staple gun, thick card, variety of clean litter, tin foil, an egg box, scissors, shredded paper, two art straws, two polystyrene spheres, length of transparent polythene, beige hessian, fabric or paper.

What to do
Cover a display box with beige coloured hessian, fabric or paper. Make a large three-dimensional 'litter bug' from rubbish. The following is just one example, but yours will obviously depend on the materials which you have available.

Cut two wing shapes from a thick piece of card. Decorate them with sweet papers and stick them to the top of a cuboid shaped box.

Cut an insect-like body shape from thick card. Draw round this body shape on another piece of card and cut it out. Decorate it with labels, wrappers, crisp packets etc. Staple the body shape round the box in front of the wings, curving it if possible.

Cut out and staple six legs to the bottom of the box. These could be pieces of card, covered in tin foil.

Stick a small, cube-shaped box as a head at the front of the body. Add egg box eyes and decorate with shredded paper or any other waste paper. Add two antennae made from art straws pushed into polystyrene spheres.

Place the 'litter bug' on to the display box and surround with litter. A litter-covered slimy trail could be added by sticking litter on to a length of transparent polythene. Add an appropriate label such as 'Are you a litter bug like this?'

Are you a litter bug like this?

Discussion

What do the children think the model is? Can they describe how and from what it is made? What is it doing?

Where should litter be put (in the classroom, playground, at home, street)? What is wrong with dropping litter on to the ground? Do they realise litter can be dangerous to people and animals?

Pupils' display

Age range

Four upwards.

What you need

Display board covered in blue backing paper, white paper, paints, chalks, scissors, variety of small pieces of clean litter, adhesive, paper for speech bubbles, sugar paper, felt-tipped pens, staple gun.

What to do

Cover a display board with blue backing paper.

Ask the children to paint large pictures of themselves. Encourage them to look at their own physical characteristics and the clothing they are wearing. When the paintings are dry, cut them out.

Give the children chalks and ask them to add small details to their paintings, such as pockets, buttons, belts, eyelashes, patterns on clothing, etc.

Allow each child to choose a piece of litter (sweet wrappers, crisp packets, labels from tins, etc) and stick it on to one of the hands in their painting.

Organise two or three children to draw a large bin on sugar paper, cut it out and stick a collage of litter on to it. Staple the litter bin on to the display board together with the paintings of children.

Add speech bubbles to some of the pictures of children: 'I am picking up litter', 'Put rubbish in the bin', etc.

Discussion

Why is chalk a good way of adding details to a painting? Are there any disadvantages? Are there any alternative ways of achieving this?

How many different kinds of litter are

there on the frieze? What materials have been used to make the bags, labels, etc? Are these materials biodegradable? Test some samples by leaving them outside over a long period.

What other kinds of litter can the children name? Are these made from materials not already discussed?

Maps

Stimulus display

Age range
Any age.

What you need
Display board and box covered in neutral colour, toy farm plus base board, large piece of white paper, scissors, staple gun, felt-tipped pens.

What to do
Arrange a toy farm on a base board on a display box. The arrangement can increase in complexity according to the age and experience of the children.

Cut a piece of white paper exactly the same size as the base board. Create a map of the farm layout by drawing round the farm buildings in the correct position. Add other details, such as green grass areas, paths, blue pond, etc. Staple this on a display board directly above the farm model.

Decide upon a list of things which you would like the children to find. Put models of these, for example a scarecrow, dog, farmer and tractor, on to the farm layout and draw simple symbols to represent them on the map.

Add a label challenging the children to find the things listed, both on the model and on the map. Picture symbols could help the youngest children.

Discussion
Allow the children time to look carefully at both the model and the map. Read the list of things which you would like them to find. Can individual children point to the 'real' thing and then the corresponding image on the map? Discuss plan views

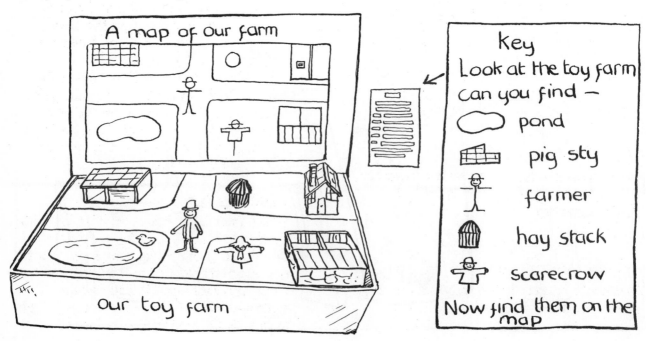

Use a map to set out the farm

our toy farm

(eg buildings, pond, paths), picture symbols (eg farmer, dog, scarecrow) and the symbolic use of colour (eg green for grass, blue for water).

This activity can be extended by changing the list of things to find or by removing the things from the model farm and asking the children to use the map to replace them.

Obviously, a similar map could be made using other standard early years equipment, such as a village playmat.

Pupils' display

Age range
Five upwards.

What you need
White paper exactly the same size as the base board, pencils, crayons, toy farm, display board and box covered in neutral colour.

What to do
Suggest the children work in pairs or small groups. Challenge them to rearrange the farm model and create their own simple map using the same techniques of drawing round buildings and adding picture symbols.

Display the finished maps and invite other children to use the map as a guide to arranging the farm model. Initially, they could place the 'real' items on top of the map and then try to place them on a separate base board.

Discussion
Which map is the easiest and which is the hardest to follow? Can the children describe any difficulties they experienced and suggest solutions to the problems? Have they managed to use colours symbolically? Are they interested enough to look at Ordnance Survey maps?

Conservation

Stimulus display

Age range
Any age.

What you need
Display board covered with dark red backing paper, adhesive, gold paper, white paper and felt-tipped pens for labels, dark blue sugar paper, shiny paper, sweet papers, gift wrapping paper, pictures (cut from magazines) of things which need 'conserving' such as endangered animals, birds and plants, trees, soil, water, buildings, etc.

What to do
Cover a display board with dark red backing paper. Staple a title to the top of the board, such as 'Guess what's inside the treasure chest'.

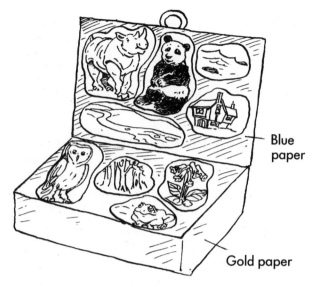

Blue paper

Gold paper

Figure 1

Make a picture of a treasure chest with a lid which can be opened. Using Figure 1 for reference, cut the two visible sides of the treasure chest out of gold paper. Cut a piece of dark blue sugar paper so that it is large enough to form the inside base of the chest and be folded over to create a lid. Decorate the lid of the chest

with jewels cut from shiny paper, sweet papers and gift wrapping paper. Cut a golden paper loop and fix it to the lid to represent a lock.

On the inside of the lid and inside the chest, stick pictures of things which are in need of conservation, such as endangered animals, birds and plants, trees, soil, water, buildings, etc. Staple the blue sugar paper to the display board.

Add another label which says 'Are we caring for the treasures of the earth?' beneath the treasure chest.

Discussion

Initially, leave the lid of the treasure chest closed and encourage the children to guess what kind of 'treasure' is in the chest. Very young children may need an explanation of the term 'treasure chest'. Pin up a piece of paper so that the pupils can record their guesses. Make a special event of opening up the treasure chest and pin the lid open on the display board. Did anyone manage to guess correctly?

Can the children name the pictures inside the treasure chest? Why is each one precious? Do they realise what kind

of danger each one is in? Discuss the problems involved in attempting to 'conserve' each one and the consequences of doing nothing. Can the pupils suggest other examples which could be added to the treasure chest?

Is there anything practical which the children can do towards conservation? They could, for example, plant cowslips in the school grounds, put up a nesting box, build a small pond, join organisations concerned with protecting wildlife, raise money for a particular conservation cause, etc.

Pupils' display

Age range

Five upwards.

What you need

Display board covered with light green backing paper, staple gun, white paper, paints, felt-tipped pen, small table covered with light green paper, vase of brambles.

What to do

Cover a display board with light green backing paper.

Make a frieze illustrating the variety of life dependent on a bramble bush. If possible, take the children to look at a bramble bush in detail. Can they name the various parts of the plant? Are there any creatures or evidence of creatures visiting the plant? Find out how many animals, birds, insects, etc, use the bramble plant as a source of food, for shelter, etc.

Take one or two pieces of the bramble plant back to the classroom. Try to include as many parts of the plant as possible.

Arrange for several children to paint brambles from observation. Encourage them to include as much detail as possible in their paintings. When the paintings are dry, cut them out and staple them to the display board. Overlap them and create a three-dimensional effect by bending some of the pieces so they stand out from the board.

Ask one child to paint a large picture of someone with shears about to cut down the bramble. When it is dry, cut it out and staple it on to the board.

Arrange for other children to paint pictures of all the creatures which they have discovered use the bramble plant. For example, bees feed on the nectar from the flowers; snails and caterpillars eat the leaves; butterflies feed on the juice from the berries; spiders attach their webs to the stems; birds, badgers, mice and people eat the berries. Whenever possible, use direct observation as a source of reference. When the individual paintings are dry, cut them out and staple them on to the bramble painting. Add an appropriate label, such as 'Who needs brambles?'

Place a vase containing sprays of bramble plant on a small table beneath the display.

Discussion

Count how many creatures are using the bramble bush and discuss why they are doing so. Why do people dislike brambles? What would happen to all the creatures dependent upon the plant if all the brambles were cut down? Discuss the need to keep some brambles because of their importance to wildlife. Is it possible to plant some in the school grounds?

Obviously, there are many other examples which could have been used instead of brambles, such as nettles, an oak tree, a pond or ditch, etc. Choose an example for which you can most easily provide firsthand experience.

History

Chapter seven

Whilst many aspects of history can provide suitable subjects for display, it is a much more difficult area to resource. Early years pupils gain considerably more understanding of history if they can handle and explore 'real' objects and this is an important point to remember when designing displays. Access to a Schools' Museum Service or a local museum can help to make this subject easier to resource. Parents or other people in the local community may also be willing to lend items.

Transport

Stimulus display

Age range
Any age.

What you need
Display board covered in grey backing paper, staple gun, black sugar paper, two pictures of vehicles (one old-fashioned, one modern), black felt-tipped pen, red and blue sugar paper, white card, two display boxes covered in grey hessian, fabric or paper, model vehicles both old-fashioned and modern (borrowed from pupils or from Schools Museum Service).

What to do
Cover a display board with grey backing paper. Cut the word 'Transport' from black sugar paper and staple it as a heading at the top of the board.

Find two large pictures or posters of vehicles, one old-fashioned and one modern. Mount the picture of the old-fashioned vehicles on red sugar paper and the one of modern vehicles on blue sugar paper. Staple these to the display board. Use a black felt-tipped pen to write 'Old' on a red sugar paper label and 'New' on a blue sugar paper label. Staple these under the appropriate picture.

Place two display boxes (covered in grey hessian, fabric or paper) beneath the board. Display models of different vehicles on the boxes; some should be modern whilst others should be obviously old-fashioned. Toy vehicles could be borrowed from the pupils or models may be obtainable from a museum (or Schools Museum Service).

Cut out a lorry-shaped cardboard pocket and staple it to the display board. Make red labels with 'Old' written on them and blue labels with 'New' written on them and put them in the pocket.

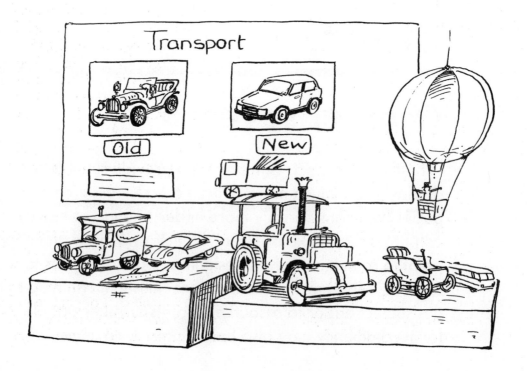

Invite the pupils to place the correct label beside each model.

Discussion

After the pupils have had some time to practise matching the labels to the models, discuss the display with them in detail. What criteria are they using to decide whether a vehicle is 'old' or 'new'? Draw their attention to the shape, colour, materials used and any writing on each vehicle. What features do the modern vehicles have which the old-fashioned ones do not? How are the vehicles powered? For example, are any horse-drawn? Which would be most comfortable to ride in and why?

Pupils' display

Age range

Five upwards.

What you need

Two toy vehicles, one old and one new, display board, red and blue sugar paper, paint, white paper, black felt-tipped pen, display box.

What to do

Choose two contrasting vehicles from the display and discuss them in detail with the pupils. What features are the same on both vehicles? What are the differences?

Organise two or three children to work together to produce a large painting of each vehicle. Encourage them to refer back to the models so that they include as much detail as possible in their paintings.

Cover half a display board with red backing paper and the other half with blue. Cut out the two paintings of vehicles and staple the old-fashioned one on to the red half of the display board and the modern one on to the blue. Add 'Old'

and 'New' labels.

Beside each vehicle, staple a large sheet of white paper, listing the features of that particular vehicle which have been highlighted by the pupils' observations. For example, 'The hansom cab has two wheels, is pulled by a horse, is made from wood, etc' and 'The Volkswagen Golf has four wheels, has an engine, is made from metal, etc'.

Display both of the model vehicles on a box beneath the display board.

Discussion

How many details have been included in the paintings of the models? Are there any important features which have been left out? Read the lists for both vehicles. Can the pupils add any more differences to either list? Which vehicle would the pupils prefer to ride in and why?

Kitchens

Stimulus display

Age range
Any age.

What you need
Two large display boxes and two or three small ones, staple gun, large piece of dark red hessian, card for labels, felt-tipped pens, collection of old household objects used in a kitchen of the nineteenth century, paper for questionnaire.

What to do
Arrange the large display boxes with the smaller ones on top. Drape the hessian over all the boxes so that a tiered effect is achieved. Anchor the hessian by stapling it to the boxes.

Display the old kitchen objects on the boxes. If possible, try to find objects from roughly the same period. A museum, local antique shop or parents may be willing to lend items. A collection could include a copper kettle, feather duster, carpet beater, flat iron, candle in candlestick, oil lamp, washboard, hot water bottle, tin bath, bellows and butter pats. Add a label saying 'These things might have been found in a kitchen 100 years ago. What do you think they were used for?'

Devise a simple questionnaire based on the objects to help direct the pupils' exploration of them. Place the questionnaires in a basket close to the display. Very young children could dictate their responses to an adult. Questions could include:
- What colour is it?
- What is it made of?
- What does it feel like?
- Does it have a smell?
- Is it heavy or light?

- What shape is it?
- Do any parts move?
- What do you think it was used for?
- How did it work?
- What would we use today instead?

Instead of a written questionnaire, the questions could be dictated on to a tape recorder which the pupils could operate whilst looking at the display.

Discussion

Allow the children plenty of time to explore the objects before introducing the questionnaire. Once they have completed the questionnaire, organise a group or class discussion to compare their answers. Were many of the pupils correct in their deductions? Had any of the pupils seen similar objects elsewhere? What advantages/disadvantages do these old objects have over modern appliances and tools (speed, efficiency, hygiene, safety, power, etc)? Do the pupils or their older relatives have other old kitchen objects at home which they could bring to school to show and discuss?

Pupils' display

Age range
Five upwards.

What you need
Display board covered in cream and beige backing paper, staple gun, black and brown sugar paper, white paper, felt-tipped pens, charcoal, collection of objects or pictures relating to kitchens 100 years ago.

What to do
Cover half the display board with cream backing paper and the other half with beige backing paper. Cut out a heading which says 'In the kitchen' from black sugar paper. Staple the heading in the middle of the board.

Staple a label 'Today' on the cream backing paper and a label '100 years ago' on the beige backing paper.

Use the objects on the stimulus display or detailed photographs as a starting point to discuss the differences between a kitchen today and one of 100 years ago. Ask the pupils to work in pairs to decide which piece of kitchen equipment they would like to illustrate.

Suggest that in each pair, one child draws the old object whilst the other draws a modern equivalent. Give brown sugar paper to the pupils drawing the old objects and white paper to those drawing the modern appliances. Ask all of the children to use charcoal for their drawings and discuss techniques such as smudging to create tone. Whenever possible, have the objects available for the children to draw from observation, for example a flat iron and a modern steam iron, an oil lamp and a modern reading lamp etc. Some pupils may be happier drawing a person using the object, whilst others may prefer to draw

the object itself.

Cut each picture out and staple on the correct half of the display board. Add labels to each one, describing what is happening, for example 'loading the washing machine' and 'using the washboard' etc.

Discussion

Have the pupils any concept of 100 years ago (for example, when their great-grandparents were alive)? Can the pupils say which half of the display board represents today and which 100 years ago? Look at each of the pictures and discuss what is happening and the objects depicted. Encourage the pupils to match the pictures on the 'Today' side of the board with their equivalents on the '100 years ago' side. Can they suggest other examples which could have been included?

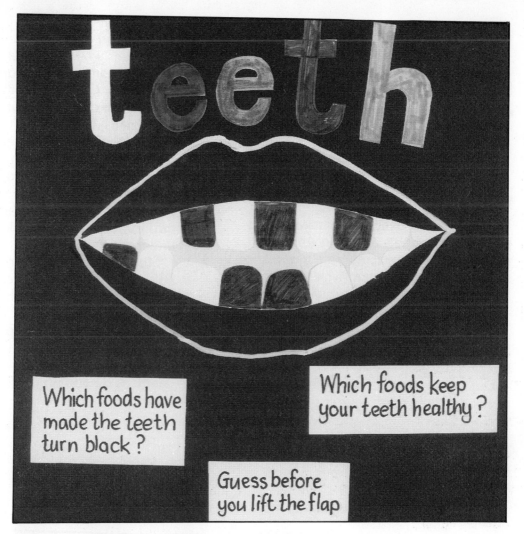

Health education

Chapter eight

Health education is an important cross-curricular theme and a popular subject for displays in early years classrooms. As well as teeth and road safety, other subjects could include general safety, 'stranger danger', exercise, diet and hygiene. Obviously, it is important to be careful not to cause unintentional distress to pupils when discussing potential sensitive areas such as weight and personal appearance. Similarly, be aware of cultural and religious preferences when organising displays about diet.

Teeth

Stimulus display

Age range
Any age.

What you need
Display board covered in black backing paper, large sheets of strong white card, felt-tipped pens, pictures from magazines, stapler, red sugar paper, white paper for labels.

What to do
Cover a display board with black backing paper.

Draw two large sets of teeth on pieces of strong white card. Colour several of the teeth on one set black and leave the remainder white. Cut round three edges of each tooth so that it can be lifted separately. On each tooth in the second set, draw a picture (or cut some from magazines) of a different food corresponding with the teeth on the first set. Make sure that when Set 1 is stapled over Set 2, foods which are good for teeth (carrots, celery etc) will appear under the white teeth, whilst food which is bad for teeth (sweets, lollies, etc) will be under the black teeth.

Staple the first set over the second. Fold along the top of each tooth to create a flap. Staple both sets of teeth to a display board.

Staple a large set of lips cut from red sugar paper around the teeth.

Cut out large white letters for the word 'teeth' as a heading at the top of the board.

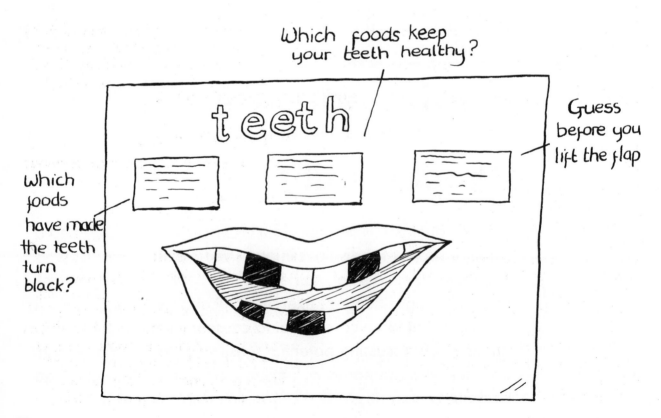

Add a label which poses a question about the teeth, for example, 'Which foods have made the teeth turn black? Which foods keep your teeth healthy? Guess before you lift the flap.'

Discussion

What colour should healthy teeth be? Why are some of the teeth black? How many black ones are there? Choose individual children to lift the tooth flap to discover the food picture underneath. Emphasise that they should try to predict which foods they think they might find. What kinds of food are found under the black teeth? Apart from eating certain foods, how else can we help to keep our teeth healthy? Discuss regular cleaning and the importance of check-up visits to the dentist.

If appropriate, use the display to reinforce the ordinal aspect of number by asking individual children to lift specific flaps. For example, you could say, 'On the top row of teeth, lift the fourth flap along from the left', etc.

Pupils' display

Age range
Four upwards.

What you need
A collection of toothbrushes, white drawing paper, pencils, felt-tipped pens, wax crayons, a variety of textured surfaces, such as wallpaper, fabric, doilies and net curtains, display board covered with pale green backing paper, bright green sugar paper, Blu-Tack, table and box covered with pale green backing

paper, a selection of items related to teeth such as toothpaste, toothbrush holder, dentist's tools and mirrors, books about teeth, etc.

What to do

Collect a variety of colourful toothbrushes for the children to draw from observation. Encourage them to draw them a lot larger than life. Allow them either to copy the colours on a particular toothbrush or invent a bright, colourful pattern of their own. Use felt-tipped pens to colour them and then cut them out.

Discuss suitable times during the day for cleaning teeth. Focus on one particular time, either morning or bedtime. Help the children to identify a logical sequence of events. For example, I get up, I wash my face, I get dressed, I eat my breakfast, I clean my teeth, I go to school.

Arrange for a group of children to draw one large picture to illustrate each stage in the sequence. Encourage them to include lots of detail by talking to them about what they would expect to find in a bathroom, bedroom, kitchen, etc.

Once the children have drawn the pictures, suggest they add textures to their pictures by making rubbings. Allow them to experiment with wax crayons and a variety of textured surfaces, such as wallpaper, fabric, doilies, net curtains, etc. This will enable them to decide which textures to use in their picture.

Mount the individual toothbrushes as a border around the edge of a display board covered in a pale green backing paper. Add a suitable heading on a giant toothbrush shape, such as 'Brush your teeth every day'.

Mount the large pictures in the correct sequence and add an appropriate label under each one. Use Blu-Tack so that they can be easily removed.

Display the toothbrushes and anything else connected with teeth (toothpaste,

dentist's tools and mirrors, books, etc) on a small table nearby.

Discussion

Play a game with the detachable labels for each picture. Remove them all, muddle them up, read each one (or ask a child to read it) and then ask a volunteer to match the correct label to the correct picture. Look carefully at the design of each toothbrush. Are all the handles the same shape? Why are some more curved than others? Which do they think would clean their teeth best and why? Are the bristles hard or soft? Why are toothbrushes usually made of plastic and not wood, metal or card? Is it a good idea to share toothbrushes?

Focus on the toothbrush border. Which is the longest toothbrush? Which is the shortest? Compare some of the others to the longest and shortest to practise 'shorter/longer than' vocabulary.

If dentist's tools are available, ask the children if they know what each instrument is used for.

Road safety

Stimulus display

Age range
Any age.

What you need
Grey backing paper, black and white paper, sugar paper, coloured squares, two different sized display boxes covered in black fabric, hessian or paper, items associated with road safety (eg fluorescent bags, bands, clothing, etc), dressmaker's dummy with lollipop person's clothing, torch.

What to do
Cover a display board with grey backing paper. Use strips of black and white paper to create a zebra crossing on the backing paper. Write a heading such as 'Cross the road safely' on to the white sections of the zebra crossing.

Cut out part of the back and front views of two vehicles. Use sugar paper and make the shapes very simple.

Leave space at the bottom of the display board for a strip of black paper with various coloured squares stuck on to it. Add a caption asking which colour shows up best against the black paper.

Place two different sized display boxes, covered in black hessian, fabric or sugar paper, in front of the board. Place items associated with road safety on to the boxes. Try to include fluorescent arm bands, bags and clothing, reflective badges, stickers and armbands.

Display a lollipop person's clothing on a dressmaker's dummy together with a lollipop sign. If possible, display a 'wand' for switching on the warning lights on one of the boxes with a notice asking the children if they know what it is used for.

Place a torch beside the display and encourage the children to shine it on to the lollipop person's clothing and the other road safety items on the display to see which colours/items show up best. (If possible, darken the area of the display slightly.)

Discussion

Discuss the correct use of a zebra crossing. What other special places are there for crossing the road safely (on a pelican crossing, with a policeman, over a footbridge, etc)? Where is it unsafe to cross the road (between parked cars)?

Discuss the role of the lollipop person and look carefully at the uniform. What materials are used and why? What colours are used and why? Ask two or three children to shine the torch on the clothing. Darken the display area if possible. Can they describe what happens? Link this with the coloured squares on the strip of black paper. Why don't lollipop people wear black uniforms? Look at the other items of safety clothing and discuss the colours and materials used. Do the pupils realise that fluorescent materials are easily seen in daylight or at dusk whereas reflective materials are best at night? Why is it important for children to wear something which makes them easily seen?

Pupils' display

Age range
Five upwards.

What you need
White drawing paper, pencils, wax crayons, black wash, sponges, cream coloured backing paper, black sugar paper, large strong cardboard box, Stanley knife, paints, long strip of fairly strong paper, two strong cardboard tubes, stapler.

What to do
Ask the children to draw either a lollipop person or a child wearing outdoor clothing. Use the dummy as a reference for those drawing the lollipop person and encourage them to look carefully at the shape and colour of the clothing. Ask one or two children to act as models wearing their outdoor clothing plus one of the fluorescent/reflective safety items from the display such as a bag or armbands. Again, focus the children's attention on the shape and colour of the clothing. Let the children colour their drawings using wax crayons. Make sure they press hard and leave no white spaces.

Allow the children to use a sponge to apply a black wash over the top of their drawing. The waxed areas should resist the paint, giving the impression of a figure in the dark.

Trim and mount the drawings on cream backing paper. Add an appropriate label, such as 'Who can be seen easily in the dark?' on two large black eye shapes.

Make a television 'film' about crossing the road safely. Use a Stanley knife to cut the appropriate holes in a cardboard box, then let two or three children paint it and add switches, aerial, cord, plug, etc.

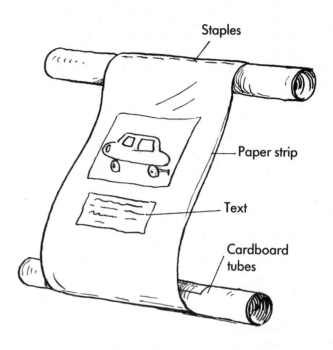

Figure 1

After discussing the important rules involved in crossing the road safely, ask for volunteers to draw pictures to illustrate each rule. Make sure the pictures will fit on to the screen and encourage the children to draw bold, bright illustrations.

Ask each child to dictate an appropriate caption for her picture which you can write on to a separate piece of white paper. Older children could, of course, do this for themselves.

Mount the pictures and text on to a long strip of paper and staple it on to two strong cardboard tubes. Wind the paper 'filmstrip' on to the tubes and then insert them into the holes in the cardboard television (Figure 1).

Place the 'television' on a table covered with cream backing paper in front of the wax resist pictures. Add a label inviting the children to watch the

television. The children could take turns to work in pairs – one gently winding on the 'filmstrip' whilst the other reads the captions to the audience.

Discussion

Encourage the children to experiment with the sponge to create different effects with the black wash and to discuss what they are doing. For example, compare dabbing it with dragging it across the paper. What happens to the paint where it touches the wax? What happens if the wax has not been applied thickly enough? Which colours show up best against the black wash?

Discuss the television filmstrip. Are there any difficulties with this design? Can the children suggest ways of overcoming these? Could they try to make their own version of a television film using slightly different techniques?

Guess what's inside each present

Lift the flap to see

RE

Chapter nine

More than any other area, RE topics such as Christmas and Harvest are perennial favourites for display and it is often difficult to find a slightly new approach to rekindle the children's interest each year. Before designing a stimulus display, it is sometimes useful to think about what significance the particular festival or celebration will have to very young children. Capture their interest by organising a display which concentrates on their point of view and then use this to draw the discussion into the more religious implications.

Christmas

Stimulus display

Age range
Any age.

What you need
Display board covered with black backing paper, staple gun, brown and grey sugar paper, white paper, felt-tipped pens, old magazines or catalogues, scissors, adhesive, Christmas wrapping paper.

What to do
Cover a display board with black backing paper. Draw a large outline of Father Christmas' sack on brown sugar paper and cut it out. Staple it on to the display board.

Draw large, simple pictures of toys, colour them with felt-tipped pens and cut them out. Alternatively, large pictures could be cut from catalogues or magazines.

Draw round each toy outline on to grey sugar paper and cut them out to produce silhouettes. Stick Christmas wrapping paper over each silhouette.

Staple the pictures of the toys on to the sack. Staple the corresponding silhouette over each picture, securing it at the top so it can be lifted like a flap.

Add an appropriate label such as 'Guess what's inside each present. Lift the flap to find out'.

Discussion
Who does the sack belong to? How many presents can the children count? Look at each present in turn. Can the children describe the shape, colour,

pattern of the paper etc? Encourage them to guess what each present might be before allowing them to lift the flap to see if they were correct. Were there any presents which were difficult to predict? Can individual children describe how each toy is used? Why do we give presents at Christmas time? Link this with the giving of gifts in the Nativity story.

Pupils' display

Age range
Four upwards.

What you need
Display board covered with backing paper, Christmas stocking filled with a variety of objects with different textures, scissors, pencils, brightly coloured sugar paper, adhesive, collage materials such as corrugated card, tissue, fabric, cotton wool, foil, string, polythene, etc.

What to do
Provide a Christmas stocking filled with objects of different shapes and textures. Encourage the children to put their hands into the stocking and feel the objects. Can they identify the objects by touch alone?

Discuss the size and shape of the Christmas stocking. Ask the children to draw a large outline of a stocking on to a piece of sugar paper. Allow them to choose the size and colour of the paper. Cut out the stocking.

Provide a variety of collage materials. Encourage the children to sort them into rough and smooth, hard and soft, etc. Ask them to cut or tear up collage materials into small pieces and stick them on to the stocking shapes.

Mount the stockings on to a display board, covered with an appropriate backing paper. Add a suitable label.

Display the real stocking, containing a new set of objects, for the children to use as a 'feelie game'.

Discussion

Have the children managed to stick shapes and textures on their collage stocking which are similar to those in the real stocking? Have they included materials which are hard, bumpy or fluffy? Suggest they shut their eyes to feel the completed stocking. Which is the softest collage material? Can they find a distinctive shape by touch alone? What kinds of presents do these shapes and textures remind them of? Encourage them to feel the new objects in the real stocking hung on the display board. Maintain interest by trying to change the objects as often as possible. Suggest that the children close their eyes and feel the collage stockings on the display board. Can they describe the textures? Compare this display with the stimulus one above. Which sense do they need to use most for each display?

Winter

Stimulus display

Age range
Any age.

What you need
Display board and two boxes covered with black paper or fabric, white paper, scissors, staple gun, posters, collection of items associated with winter, spray snow.

What to do
Cover a display board and two display boxes with black paper or fabric. Cut out a heading from white paper which says 'Signs of winter'. Staple posters on a wintery theme on to the display board.

These could include pictures of snowflakes, icicles, snowy landscapes, snowmen or birds and animals in winter.

Arrange a collection of items associated with winter on the two display boxes. This could include a vase with bare twigs; dead leaves of various shapes, colours and sizes; different kinds of fir cones, a bowl of evergreen plants; hyacinth bulbs suspended over water in jam jars.

Use Christmas snow spray to create a snowy effect.

Discussion

What signs of winter can the pupils see in the posters? Look carefully at each item on the display box. Can the pupils describe each one using all their senses? What is the difference between deciduous and evergreen plants? What plants and animals seem to be 'sleeping' in winter and why does this happen? Can the pupils predict what will happen to the hyacinth bulbs? Are these a sign of winter or spring?

Pupils' display

Age range
Four upwards.

What you need
Grey, light green and dark blue sugar paper, white paint, items for printing (for example, corks, cardboard tubes, balsa wood, shampoo lids, newspaper, sponges), brightly coloured paints, brushes, staple gun, scissors, posters/photographs/picture books of snowmen.

What to do
Organise several children to print snowflakes with white paint on dark blue sugar paper. Offer them a range of implements with which to print, such as corks, cardboard tubes, balsa wood, plastic shampoo lids, etc.

Arrange for a second group of children to print a snowy texture on light green sugar paper to represent snow-covered ground. Can they suggest an

appropriate technique (such as using screwed up newspaper)?

Staple the blue sugar paper to the display board. Cut the light green 'ground' into gently curving shapes and staple it so that it overlaps the sky.

It will probably be difficult to provide first-hand observation of a snowman, so secondary sources such as posters, photographs, picture books, etc, will need to be available. Discuss the shapes and sizes of the snowmen and focus especially upon any accessories such as hats, scarves, gloves, etc. Invite the children to draw a simple outline of a snowman on grey sugar paper. Ask them to sponge print white paint all over the snowman's body. Offer them brightly coloured paints and encourage them to paint further details, such as a hat, scarf, buttons, eyes, nose, mouth, etc.

When the snowmen are dry, cut them out and staple them on to the background. A three-dimensional effect can be achieved by bending the snowmen as they are stapled on to the board.

Add an appropriate label, such as 'Can you build a snowman?'.

Discussion

How many different implements were used for printing? Which were successful and which were not? Which implements achieved similar textures? Can the children suggest alternative subject matters for some of the implements? Could the sponges be used to create a misty sky? Is each snowman unique? How are they similar or different? Would the frieze have been so interesting if all the snowmen had been identical?

What other activities do the children enjoy doing in the snow? What do they like or dislike about the snow? Are there any people who might not like the snow? How can we help make life easy for them in cold weather?

Harvest

Stimulus display

Age range
Any age.

What you need
Display board covered in dark green backing paper, display box covered in dark green hessian, fabric or paper, scissors, staple gun, bright yellow paper, black felt-tipped pens, white paper, poster of bees, products associated with bees such as flowers, a jar of honey, fruit, honey-based foods, beeswax polish, honeycomb candles, etc.

What to do
Cover a display board with dark green backing paper. Cut out the word 'Bees' from bright yellow paper, adding black stripes to each letter. Staple the word as a heading to the display. Write 'Small but IMPORTANT' on yellow paper and staple it towards the bottom of the board.

Staple a poster illustrating honey bees in the middle of the board. Add two yellow arrows, pointing outwards from either side of the poster. On the left hand side of the poster, add a label saying 'pollinate flowers' together with a picture of some flowers. On the right hand side of the poster, add a label saying 'make honey' together with a cut out shape of a jar of honey.

Draw, colour and cut out small, simple pictures of bees, then staple them on to the display.

Place two display boxes (covered in dark green hessian, fabric or paper) beneath the board. Add a label saying 'Without bees, we would not have . . .' and arrange a collection of objects to illustrate this, such as flowers, fruit, a jar of honey, honey-based foods, beeswax polish, honeycomb candles, etc.

Discussion

Can the children identify the bees? What do they know about them? Younger children will need an explanation about pollination and the production of honey,

but older children may well have some knowledge. Through discussion, ensure they understand the important role played by bees. Can they identify any of the products on the display box and say why bees are associated with them? Do they realise that this is a harvest from bees just as there is a harvest from corn? Emphasise the importance of this tiny insect and compare it to the children's own contribution to the class, school and their family.

Pupils' display

Age range

Four upwards.

What you need

Display board covered with pale blue backing paper, staple gun, bunch of flowers, white paper, paint, scissors, dead bee, magnifying glasses, buff coloured sugar paper, charcoal, pastels or chalks.

What to do

Cover a display board with pale blue backing paper. Show the children several different kinds of flowers and discuss their colour, shape, size, structure, etc. Ask the children to choose one flower to paint. Offer the children two distinct sizes of paper to choose from and suggest they paint their flower as tall as the piece of paper.

Whilst they are painting, encourage them to refer back to their flower and to include as many details as possible. Is the stem straight or curved? Is it hairy or smooth? Are the petals all the same colour?

When the paintings are dry, cut out each flower and staple them on to the display board. Bend and twist the flowers as you staple them to create a three-dimensional effect.

Show the children a dead bee and allow them to look at it closely through magnifying glasses. Discuss its shape,

colour and structure. It may also help to have posters or pictures of bees to supplement this discussion.

Give each child a piece of buff coloured sugar paper and charcoal and ask them to draw a large bee based on their observations. Through discussion, encourage them to include details.

Offer them yellow or orange pastels or chalks so they can add an appropriate body colour if they wish.

Cut out the bees and staple them on to the flowers.

Add an appropriate label such as 'Buzz, buzz, buzz. Bees give us honey'.

Discussion

How have the children's observations of bees and flowers improved their pictures? Would they have found it easy to draw without looking? What new discoveries have they made about bees and flowers as a result of looking closely at them?